WOMEN, CRIME AND LAW

About the Editor

Dr Ranga Ranjan Das, one of the emerging researchers of the north eastern region who nicely capitalize his theoretical understandings of several social science disciplines in exploring north eastern societies in multiple dimensions. He is working beyond his professional legacy of law research to unravel real situation of the north east. He is a prolific writer in several inter-disciplinary approaches along with creative vernacular literatures. He has edited several north eastern volumes, writes research papers and popular articles for edited volumes, journals and popular volumes. At present, he is professionally associated with Law Research Institute of Gauhati High Court, Guwahati.

Women, Crime and Law

Editor
Dr Ranga Ranjan Das

Akansha Publishing House
Delhi • Guwahati • Visakhapatnam

AKANSHA PUBLISHING HOUSE
4649-B/21, Ansari Road
Daryaganj, New Delhi-110002
Phones: 23263193 / 9811582579 / 09435116718
Fax: 011-23263193
Email: ektabooks@yahoo.com
visit us: www.akanshapublishinghouse.com

Women, Crime and Law

First Published 2021

ISBN 978-81-8370-586-8

PRINTED IN INDIA

Published by Akansha Publishing House, New Delhi-110002 and printed in India.

Preface

Emerging legal research perspectives pointed out multidimensional issues and concerns in India general and north eastern region in particular. Out of such one issue that often come across is women-why and how in Indian context woman become victim of gross violence, atrocity and crime. Why the statistics of National Crime Records Bureau (NCRB) shows increasing trends on the crime against women in every year? Scholars pointed out that the real scenario is completely different. Statistics of the bureau is based upon the reported crime that means local police authority has got apprehension about such incidents, victims and accused. The law of the country has also provided landmark judgments' against the accused in recent times.

Why a woman is victimized in the country? There are several opinions put forwarded by different jurists, lawmakers, scholars and authors. Out of these the patriarchal mindset, perhaps one of the key reasons. There has been long history. It also provides another thought where we found woman is at the apex of kingdom, woman as a freedom fighter, martyr and socio-political scenario. If we observe the contemporary Indian woman, they are marching forward parallel to their male counterpart, even some steps ahead in certain cases.

The civilization of India has a glorious past where woman has been worshipped in the form of various goddesses and deities. It is still continuing. What happens when it comes to present societal set up? Why we forget the role of woman as mother, sister, wife and torch bearer of culture who not only the shapes a family but also play an active role in the mobilization of entire society. We have our Constitutional mandates and stringent laws under various Acts, enactments and sections under Indian Penal Codes. It is found that people has different perceptions about such acts and laws. For example, we have dowry prohibition act, but still custom of dowry is going on through negotiation between the intending families in an expressive or suppressive way. So we often come across the dowry related cases. There are several other cases like rape, murder, acid attack where woman becomes victim in Indian context. We are living in the era of globalization and digitalization. There are gross positive and negative impacts of new devices that modern generation carries in their pocket. What is their thought process? Whether they can adjust with the technological intervention in proper way? What prompts the man/youth (male) to commit crime, violence or atrocities against girl/women? Whether they don't have any fear of legal consequences? There are several pertinent questions. It can be sorted out by bottom to top approach- not from top-bottom approach. What is the environment of our families? Whether a growing youth inculcate the good social values of family or not? There are lots of important steps to be taken by the contemporary Indian families. It is also seen that earlier we have a system of 'joint family system where members' are confined under strict rules. In some places it is still continued. Due to present and changing economic scenario, joint families are broken into nuclear families and compete for earning materialistic wealth at any cost. There is perhaps an impact on upbringing in different family context.

It is not accurate to generalize all male as enemy of woman who has been alleged as perpetrators of crime, violence and atrocities. Out of these there are some who are convicted.

Case studies of such convicts, their approach and family background will provide us valuable feedback to ascertain certain conclusions pertaining to their criminal behaviour. Criminal psychology may perhaps play a crucial role.

Under such circumstances, the book is an attempt to bring divergent areas of thought emphasizing the various dimensions of crimes, atrocities and violence against woman from past to contemporary times. It is an outcome of sincere efforts of a handful of young and bright scholars from legal and social science background who put forward their valuable observations incorporating and analyzing data from the NCRB considering it as one of the most sensitive issue in contemporary India. Sincerity and hard work always pays. We, would like to thank to all the contributors for this volume. Besides, we offer our sincere thanks to Parashmoni Bordoloi and Jitul Kalita for their relentless effort while preparing the book. In spite of our best efforts, there may remain some incorrect facts and statistical figure, incorrect interpretation of circumstances, situations in the body of the text. We need valuable advice and necessary suggestions from the readers to rectify in due course. We also appreciate and acknowledge the academic and research bonding with M.P. Misra, of Akansha Publishing House, New Delhi for bringing out the volume in quick time. Hope the volume will beneficial for the all the readers in general and those associated with law, woman organizations, social science researchers in particular.

RANGA RANJAN DAS

Contents

Contributors

1. Adrita Bhuyan, Assam, 9577075599, adrita.bhuyan@yahoo.com

2. Anshumi Chowdhury, Tamulichuburi, Mazgaon, Tezpur, Assam, Pin 784001, Phone, 9706032595, canshumi95@gmail.com

3. Hemen Saud, village and PO: Niz Pakowa, Dist. Nalbari, Assam, Pin 781353, Phone: 9101828354, saudhemen1993@gmail.com

4. Monjushna Goswami, Amolapatty Near Natya Mandir, Nagaon, Assam, Pin 702003, Phone 7002886843, meghagoswami56@gmail.com

5. Pallabi Goswami, House No 4, Kamala-Bimalaloy, Near Riscon Enclave, Hockey Stadium Road, Sawkuchi, Guwahati 781040, Phone-7016405974, pallavigoswami98@gmail.com

6. Sarthak Arora, Phone: 9999343408, email: sarthakaroraadv@gmail.com

7. Shubhank Gour, School of Law, Devi Ahilya Vishvavidhyalaya (DAVV), Indore, Madhya Pradesh

8. Soyonika Gogoi, Club Road, Chekonidhara Hari Mandir Path, Jorhat-785001, Assam, 9886424192, soyonikagogoi@gmail.com

9. Suhavi Arya, Guwahati, 9910522249, suhaviarya@gmail.com

10. Vaibhav Kumar Garg, 2270/2nd Floor, Sector 28, HBC, Faridabad, Haryana (India), 8587097907, gargvaibhav.sk@gmail.com

11. Yash Singh Sisodiya, 9826044452, yashwardhan423@gmail.com

1

Introduction

Crime, Women and Law: Global Perspectives and National Dimensions

Ranga Ranjan Das

"There is a role for leadership and legislators to make violence against women illegal and to punish offenders. Many countries already have appropriate laws in place, but they are not fully enforced. That has to change. States have a primary role to play in implementing current laws and conventions, and in introducing new legislations where it is lacking".

Phumzile Mlambo-Ngcuka, UN Women Executive Director

Crime *vis-à-vis* violence pertaining to women is one of the serious issues in the current times. The United Nations defines violence against women as, 'any act of gender-based violence that results in, or is likely to result in physical, sexual or mental harm or suffering to women, including threats of such acts, coercion or arbitrary deprivation of liberty, whether occurring in public or in private life.[1] Violence often transformed as crime in the eye of law. What is crime? Dictionary[2] generalizes the meaning of 'crime' as any activities that involve breaking the law. Again what is law about? It is the whole system of rules that everyone in a country or society must obey. Crime perspectives have several causes and consequences. There are many push and pull factors associated with crime. Our analysis of crime takes place after it is happened. Emphasis is made upon nature of crime, individual involved and statistics. We are not interpreting the various forces and factors leading to crime. Every country has own laws, device or mechanism in the form of stringent punishment to check the crime. Are we sure that such mechanism is really effective for minimizing the crime rate. As society advances with neo-technological achievement, the definition and meaning of crime switches from physical crime to virtual crime in the form of cyber-crime. An overview of crime scenario at global perspectives shows that there are several acts executed by individual or groups-that is against law-that not only cause physical or financial damage leading to death but also affects a country. The acts relating to human such as assault, rape, murder, stealing, thief, dacoity, human trafficking, smuggling of various items like gold, monuments, narcotic substances, illegal weapons, abduction and kidnapping for ransom, conspiracy against state or nation, abetment for communal riots, suicide, fraud, cheating, forgery, illegal transplantation of organ, determination of sex before birth, death related to dowry, organized crime related to woman, corruption, white collar crime, money laundering, cyber-attacks, etc. Any crimes may affect both male and female. Where there is crime, there is criminal. It may be a man or a woman. Most of the observation asserts that it is man who executes most of the crime. In the present day world, it is always important to trace out the mastermind behind any crime to locate gender. The prisons of the various parts of the world have spaces for woman also. If we analysis the crime scenario, its' nature and involvement, an interesting feature comes out. There are increasing trend of crimes associated specifically with woman. Such increasing rates compel the states to frame specific laws relating to woman.

GLOBAL PERSPECTIVES

Crime, violence and injustice against woman are worldwide phenomena. Execution, nature and content differ from one country to another but there are common elements. Rape, other sexual offences, trafficking is there besides woman has to face violence by intimate partners. It is estimated that 35 per cent of woman across the world have experienced either physical and/ or sexual intimate partner violence or sexual violence by a non-partner at some point in their lives.[3] Global scenario can be assessed in the assertion when Ngcuka[4] (2020) observes the situation of woman during the lockdown period:

> "As more countries report infection and lockdown, more domestic violence help lines and shelters across the world are reporting rising calls for help. Confinement is fostering the tension and strain created by security, health and money worries. And it is increasing isolation for women with violent partners, separating them from the people and resources that can best help them. Even before covid-19 existed, domestic violence was already one of the greatest human rights violations. In the previous 12 months, 243 million women and girls (aged 15-49) across the world have been subjected to sexual or physical violence by an intimate partner. As the covid 19 pandemic continues, this number is likely to grow with multiple impacts on women's well-being".

In every situation, woman is victim whether from insiders, outsiders or dictators to dominant their voices. In the recent history the assassination of the Mirabel sisters of the Dominican Republic on November 25, 1960 was an eye-opener for the whole world. These three courageous sisters-Patria, Maria and Minerva-who were also known as Las Mariposas, stood firm against the oppressive dictatorial regime of Rafael Trujillo in the Dominican Republic. It was in 1999 that the United Nations decided to designate November 25 as the International Day for Elimination of Violence against Women and decided to observe a whole fortnight beginning November 25 every year as a period of activism against gender violence across the globe.[5] Apart from crime and against the raising voice of gender equality, conservative societies of different countries possess own stereotype vision at their own backward. For example in Egypt five women is awarded 14 lacs as fine and two years of imprisonment for exclusive use of tiktok in recent times.[6]

It is not about law but mindset of the people how they react. Government can amend laws by increasing quantum of punishment for criminals but we have to search impinging factors that effects to change our mindset. Changes in law are happening across the world. For example, increasing number of rape cases in Bangladesh compel to approve amendment on the Women and Children Repression Prevention Act that elevate the maximum punishment from life imprisonment to death in rape cases. It has happened due to protest staged by different organizations at Dhaka's Shahbagh square and other parts of the country against sexual assaults on a woman. It gets intensified due to the incidents at Noakhali and Sylhet's MC College. According to statistics provided by Tribunals, as many as 4541 rape cases have been reported in Bangladesh in the past 16 years and only 60 are convicted. During the current 2020 year, 889 women are raped between January and August as asserted by Rights Group Ain O Salish Kendra. There are 192 others who faced attempted rapes and sexual harassment during the period, nine of the victims committed suicide. Human rights activists do not deny the possibilities of increasing numbers as most of the victims hesitate to lodge complain to the police.[7] Rape has an overwhelming impact not only woman but also entire humanity. Why is it taking places? Feminist referred the term 'rape culture'. In this regard, there is an important interpretation on rape culture that notes,

> "ever since the American feminists coined the term rape culture in the 1970s, it has been a topic of contention. The concept has often been criticized for being too women-centric, for ignoring the sexual victimization of men and for blaming the cultural norms for triggering rape rather than holding the actual perpetrators accountable. However, I beg to differ with the critics and would reckon that rape culture is not a fallacy and is indeed the contribution of the pernicious patriarchal norms that have been guiding our society since times immemorial".[8]

It, further adds,

> "It is an inconvenient truth that patriarchal norms have instilled in humans a distorted mentality, created delusional gender roles, promoted gender inequality, and gave men the entitlement to systematically harass women and have power over their life. The values and ideas nested in the imperious and dynamic web of patriarchy have always had an unprecedented appeal among all genders that has made patriarchy sustainable. These patriarchal norms did not only subjugate women but also limited the self-expression of men and undermined their vulnerability. It is these very norms and values that are addressed through the usage of the term rape culture. Rape culture does not imply rape *per se*, i.e. it is not just about the physical intrusion of a women's body. The term is used to highlight the age-old belief and response systems embedded in our culture that trivializes sexual violence and justifies denigration of humans"[9].

As a resident of human society often referred as "civilized society", our determination should be to abolish rape culture from the earth so that we retain the distinction between human and animal society.

NATIONAL DIMENSIONS AND LEGAL IMPLICATIONS

In the era where woman is marching parallel to their man's counterpart, or sometimes a step forward, it is irony to emphasis on crime against women, rape culture and gender injustice. Law has taken its' own course adhering to Constitutional mandate in India. The state has enacted various laws and taken measures intended to ensure equal rights, check social discrimination and various forms of violence and atrocities. Although woman may be victims of any of the general crimes such as murder, robbery, cheating, etc. only the crimes which are directed specifically against woman, i.e, gender specific crimes are characterized as 'crimes against woman'. New legislations have been brought and amendments have been made in existing laws to tackle such crimes effectively. These are broadly classified under two categories: crime heads under Indian Penal Code (IPC) and crime heads under the special and local laws SLL. There are different natures of crimes dealt under different IPC sections such as rape (376), attempt to commit rape (376/511), kidnapping and abduction of Women (363, 364, 364A, 365, 366 to 369) for purposes like murder, ransom, to compel for marriage and for other purposes, dowry Deaths (304 B), assault with intent to outrage her modesty (354), sexual harassment (354A), assault to outrage her modesty (354C), voyeurism (354D), others to insult to the modesty of women (509) at office premises, at places related to work, in public transport and in other places, cruelty by husband or his relatives (498 A), importation of girl from foreign country (up to 21 years of age) (366 B) and abetment of suicide of woman (306). Besides, IPC sections, there are crime heads under the special and local laws (SLL) that are enacted for protection and safety of women. It includes: Dowry Prohibition Act 1961, Indecent Representation of Women (Prohibition) Act, 1986, The Commission of Sati Prevention Act, 1987, The Protection of Woman from Domestic Violence Act, 2005 and the Immemorial Traffic (prevention) Act, 1956. The increasing crimes during post-Independent period lead to establishment of National Crime Records Bureau (NCRB) that has been providing crime statistics over the years. There is a statistics from 2011 to 2015 in an annual report entitled 'Crime in India' [10]. The facts and figure however, varies from 2016-2019 (*see* Table at page 8).

In Indian context, there are several rape incidents that came to lime light in the recent times: the rape and murder of Hathras and Unnao in Uttar Pradesh, Nirbhaya in Delhi and Kathua in Jammu. There are many other incidents that are less focused. One such example is Ms. Negi inhabitant of West Delhi. It had happened in February 9, 2012. She was kidnapped, taken to Haryana where there was gang rape and brutally killed. Body is found from agricultural field at Rudhai village of Rewari district. Rapist is convicted and ordered death punishment in 2014. But it is still pending in the Supreme Court.[11] In some point of delayed judicial process and lope holes in the law provide some encouragement. But time has changed. Every criminal will be punished very quickly according to new arrangements.

Recent trends reflect that people is hardly afraid of legal provisions. They are moving ahead. NCRB statistics make India a high-risk nation for women. It is noted that, "the 66th edition of 'Crime in India' report for the year 2018 is a testament to India's categorization as a high-risk nation for women. The report stated that the crime rate against women in India stands at 58.8% and the conviction rate for those crimes is a meager 19%. The report revealed that every 4.4

SI No.	Crime Head	Year				
		2011	2012	2013	2014	2015
1	Rape	24,206	24,923	33,707	36,735	34,651
2	Attempt to commit rape	-	-	-	4,232	4,434
3	Kidnapping and abduction of women	35,565	38,262	51,881	57,311	59,277
4	Dowry death	8,618	8,233	8,083	8,455	7,634
5	Assault on women with intent to outrage her/ their modesty	42,968	45,351	70,739	82,235	82,422
6	Insult to the modesty of women	8,570	9,173	12,589	9,735	8,685
7	Cruelty by husband or his relatives	99,135	1,06,527	1,18,866	1,22,877	1,13,403
8	Importation of girl from foreign country	80	59	31	13	6
9	Abetment of suicide of women	-	-	-	3,734	4,060
A	**Total IPC Crime against women**	2,19,142	2,32,528	2,95,896	3,25,327	3,14,575
10	Commission of Sati Prevention Act	0	0	0	0	0
11	Indecent Representation of Women (P) Act	453	141	362	47	40
12	The Dowry Prohibition Act	6,619	9,038	10,709	10,050	9,894
13	Protection of Women from Domestic Violence Act	-	-	-	426	461
14	Immoral Traffic (Prevention) Act	2,436	2,563	2,579	2,070	2,424
B	**Total SLL Crime Against Women**	9,508	11,742	13,650	12,593	12,819
	Total (A +B)	2,28,650	2,44,270	3,09,546	3,37,922	3,27,394

minutes a woman in India is subjected to an act of domestic violence and four women are raped every hour. 109 children get sexually abused every day in India of which 99% are girls.[12] Recent report[13] asserts that during 2019, 4,05,861 cases of crime against women were registered, showing an increase of 7.3% over 2018 (3,78,236 cases). Majority of cases under IPC were registered under 'cruelty by husband or his relatives' (30.9%) followed by 'assault on women with intent to outrage her modesty' (21.8%), 'kidnapping and abduction of women' (17.9%) and 'rape' (7.9%). The crime rate registered per lacs woman population is 62.4 in 2019 in comparison with 58.8 in 2018. According to 2019 report, the country had reported 88 rape cases every day and 32,033 in the year. Rajasthan and Uttar Pradesh top the shame list with 6000 and 3,065 rape cases last year respectively. [14]

It is of serious concern and a matter of deep thought. Interpreting reason and remedies, an Editorial[15] opined:

> "Failure of the government machinery apart, growing commodification of women following the infotainment boom is also having an impact on crimes against women. Then, a decadent, corrupt and highly materialistic culture bereft of values is having a huge impact on crimes against women. According to social scientists, such phenomena are always more pronounced in underdeveloped, half-educated societies where women have traditionally been accorded a second class treatment in diverse spheres starting from homes to workplaces. A society where women do not feel secure cannot at all be called a civilized society. Poor enforcement of laws aimed at tackling crimes against women cannot be viewed in isolation of the abysmal level of gender sensitization of our public functionaries-something that is compounding the plight of the victimized women. While enforcement is a must to tackle crimes

against women, any long-term strategy to fight the scourge has to hit at the deep-rooted societal prejudices that regard woman as inferior to man and reduces her to a mere commodity. An enabling home environment where male members are taught to respect women has to be the first step towards effecting lasting societal changes. Addressing the issues of gender-related inequity and poor development indices for women must be accorded priority as a matter of policy. Skewed gender indices reveal areas of concern such as adverse sex ratio, low female life expectancy rates, high fertility rates, illiteracy, etc, where women are left in a vulnerable position. Women's access to healthcare, education and employment continues to be alarmingly low in some of the parts of the country. It is this disadvantageous position that makes women susceptible to different forms of violence. If the women are to be ensured their rightful status in society, it is imperative that a forward looking and dynamic gender policy is put in place, besides of course, strengthening the law enforcing system. The policy must outline a set of proactive interventions and create the environment and receptivity required for it to be successful".

The editorial blames failure of government machinery, growing commodification of women and infotainment boom for increasing crimes against women. Across the countries, there is strong mechanism to check the crime. But crimes are taking place in one way or the other. In India also crimes especially against women is increasing day by day. We have the numbers that is provided by ncrb and also reported by media. NCRB gets the number according to police records. Nongovernment records and studies reveal that there are many such crimes against woman specially 'rape' that never comes to the notice of police and media. Accused somehow manage the situation after execution. Again, there are vast differences between the numbers of cases reported and number of persons convicted. In this regard, Bikas Khanna (2020:6) put pertinent questions and explores ground realities. Looking into Indian situation, it reveals "why Indian daughters continue to be violated despite the government framing tough anti-rape legislation? The laws do not seem to have any deterrent on the rapists as the number suggest. Every 16 minutes, a woman is raped somewhere in India". It further elaborates when he says, "majority of the crimes against women are committed by people known to the victims such as close family members, neighbours, employers and friends. And in many cases, the victims either remain reluctant to report crimes or they are coerced by their families to keep mum due to stigma attached with it. India's deep-seated patriarchy is largely to be blamed for this sorry state of affairs . . . the government was forced to pass a tough anti-rape law in April 2013 . . . and introduced the death sentence for convicted rapists. But has it brought about any positive change in the society? The young girls and women continue to fall prey to the rapists. In several cases, the accused get away with minor punishment due to lack of evidence, and they are also protected by police or politicians. The misuse of police in destroying evidence is not something a hidden secret". There are some ground realities pertaining to this observation. How to overcome such a situation? We have to re-interpret contemporary Indian society. Contrary to it, tribal societies have less such cases. In the north east, except Assam, other states have less such cases. It is pertinent to mention here that most of the hilly states have a strong mechanism of self-governance adhering customary laws and practices. Strong deterrent punishment embedded in the customary laws perhaps the reason for less number of rape cases. They resolve such cases with their own.

It is the high time to review the rest of societies. We have satisfaction of inhabiting in a more civilized, ultra-modern and hi-tech materialistic society. There are other sides of such presumption. Dowry practice is still prevalent in spite of Dowry Prohibition Act. There are some sort of mutual understandings in certain situation for providing adequate safeguards. It provides the base for emergence of crime. Further, there are certain other issues. One can look into the Indian situation in different perspectives. It is the second highest populace country where most people are young. First question is whether we are able to mobilize such rich human resources? How an adult young and male passes the entire day beyond study and work? Are we able to trace out the resources what are sources of income for the people beyond job and business? How the present generations utilize the access to internet? How can they react when they explore aged-bars videos? How much parents provides time and inculcate value-based teachings? It is also important to analysis the socio-economic and family background of the accused who are convicted for committing crime against women. Such interpretation helps to find out the connecting factor among the convicts. Criminal behaviour is a different kind of mental set up that varies according to offence. Sometimes intoxication habits cause disturbances to family life and causes inmate violence. Whether we are able to close such resources? There are also instances where woman itself is the enemy for woman. In most of the human trafficking cases and dowry related cases, involvement of women is explored. Along with nation building process, it is also imperative to restructure and reorient the mind of the people in a more constructive way so that people takes appropriate care their opposite counterpart to make a proper balance in the society.

END NOTES

1. Who.int/news-room/fact-sheets/detail/violence-against-women/facts-and-figures, visited on 14th October, 2020 at 3.45 pm

2. *New Oxford Advanced Learner's Dictionary*, AS Hornby, Seventh Edition, Oxford University Press
3. Unwomen.org/en/what-we-do/ending-violence-against-women/facts-and-figures, visited on 14th October, 2020 at 4.05 pm
4. Phumzile Mlambo-Ngcuka, Executive Director, UN Women, posted April 6, 2020, unwomen.org/en/news/stories/2020/4/statement-ed-phumzile-violence-against-women-during-pandemic, retrieved on 14th October, 2020, at 5.15 pm
5. Tapati Baruah Kashyap (2016, December 14) 'Reality of violence against women', *The Assam Tribune*, Guwhati
6. 'Five women is awarded two years imprisonment, and fine of 14 lacs in Egypt', (2020, July 29), *Axomiya Pratidin*, Vernacular Daily, Guwahati
7. 'Death for rape cases in Bangladesh', (2020, October 13), *The Assam Tribune*, English Daily, Guwahati
8. Gargi Garima Kalita (2020, June 6) "Who deserves to be blamed?', *The Sentinal*, English Daily, Guwahati, p. 6
9. ibid no 8
10. Ncrb.gov.in/sites/default/files/crime_in_india_table_additional_table_chapter_reports/chapter%205-15.11.16_2015.pdf
11. 'Kiran Negi' (2020, October 13), Editorial, *Axomiya Pratidin*, Vernacular Daily, Guwahati
12. ibid no 9
13. Ncrb.gov.in/en/crime-india, visited on 16th October, 2020 at 10.05 pm
14. Vikas Khanna (2020, October 16), 'Why stringent laws have failed to instill fear in rapists?', *The Assam Tribune*, Guwahati
15. 'Crimes against women', (2019, October 22) Editorial, *The Assam Tribune*, English Daily, Guwahati, p.6

2

Women and Crime: A Brief Review in Indian Context

Hemen Saud

Centuries have come and centuries have gone, but the plight of women is not likely to change. Time has helplessly watched women suffering in the form of discrimination, oppression, exploitation, degradation, aggression, humiliation. Indian women through the countries remained subjugated and apprised because society believed in clinging on the orthodox beliefs for the brunt of violence-domestic as well as public, physical, emotional and mental. Crimes against women are a social menace and a costly public health problem. It can take the form of threats, verbal abuse, battering, rape and murder. It is an escalating pattern of coercive behaviors' that includes physical, sexual and psychological assaults. It can explode anywhere, anytime and within any economic class. Violence against women is simply not a women's right issue, but a human right issue.

In the ancient Indian times, women held a high place of respect in the society as mentioned in Rigveda and other scriptures. There are large narratives about the status of our women and their heroic deeds from the Vedic period to the modern times. Later on due to social, political and economic changes, women lost their status. Many evil customs and traditions stepped in which enslaved the women and tied them to the boundaries of the house. Physical, sexual and psychological violence spread like epidemic worldwide. It crosses every social and economic class, every religion, race and ethnicity. From domestic abuse to rape as a weapon of war, violence against women is a gross violation of their human right. Violence happens everywhere including India. In Indian context, the crimes in which a woman is specially targeted to be harmed are characterized as 'Crime against women'. These are classified under two categories: crime under the Indian Penal Code (IPC) and crime under special and local laws.

Crime against women is defined as direct or indirect physical or mental cruelty to women. Crimes which are specially directed against women and in which the women are victims are termed as crime against women. Crime against women are of various types as crimes involving sex for economic gain including prostitution, keeping of brothel seduction, wrongful confinement, trafficking, dowry extortion murder, crime relating to women's property which includes dishonest misappropriation, criminal breach of trust, extortion, robbery and murder, crimes in relation to sex including outraging the modesty of women, use of criminal force, assault, kidnapping, abduction wrongful confinement, rape trafficking, adultery, murder, other immoral acts injuries to the society and other injuries acts against women.

The United Nations defined 'violence against women' in 1993 in its' declaration on the elimination of violence against women. It is defined as any act of gender biasness violence that results in or is likely to result in, physical, sexual or psychological harm or suffering to women, including threats of such acts, coercion on arbitrary deprivation of liberty, whether occurring in public or private life. The term violence is actually applied to physically striking an individual resulting in an injury, striking a person with the intent of causing harm but not actually causing it. In Indian situation, the expression of Constitution has lots of concern for women. Gender equality is enshrined in every sphere of Indian Constitution, be it preamble fundamental rights, fundamental duties and directive principles. The Constitution of India not only grants equality to women but also empowers the state to adopt measures of positive discrimination in favour of women for neutralizing the cumulative socio economic, education and political disadvantages faced by them. Fundamental right among others, ensure equality before the law and equal protection of law; prohibits discrimination against any citizen on grounds of religion, race, caste, sex or place of birth and guarantee equality or opportunity to all citizen in matters relating to employment. India has also ratified various international convention and human right instruments committing to secure equal rights of women. Specific Constitutional provisions for women: Equality before law for women (Article 14), state make any special provision in favour of women and children (Article 15), state not to discriminate against any citizen grounds only of religion, race, caste, sex, place of birth or any of them (Article 15) and state to raise the level of nutrition and the standard of living of its people (Article 47).

Constitutional provisions apart, there are many other legal provisions in different acts, women specific special laws and also found in different sections of Indian Penal Codes, that provide remedies and protect women. Under Factories Act, 1948, 'a woman cannot be forced to work beyond 8 hours and prohibits employment of women except between 6 am to 7 pm, under Maternity Benefit Act, 1961, 'a woman is entitled 12 weeks maternity leave with full wages', under the Dowry Prohibition Act, 1961, 'demand of dowry either before marriage, during marriage and after the marriage is an offence', Child Marriage Restrain Act, 1976 raises the age for marriage of a girl to 18 years from 15 years and that of a boy to 21 years, Medical Termination of Pregnancy Act, 1971 safeguards women from unnecessary and compulsory abortions, Protection of Women from Domestic Violence Act, 2005 protects women from any conduct omission/ commission that harms, injures on potential to harm is to be considered as Domestic Violence and Protection of Women against Sexual Harassment at Work Place Bill, 2010 aims to protect the women at work place. Explanation and punishment of various crimes are specifically mentioned in various sections of IPC such as rape (376), kidnapping and abduction (363-373), dowry death (302, 304 B), assault on woman with intent to outrage her modesty (354) and importation of girls from foreign countries (366 B). If one makes a close look on the data provided in 'Crimes in India' report of National Crime Records Bureau from 2001 to 2019, it is found that there is an increasing trend on the crime against women in Indian context in spite of Constitutional and various other legislative provisions.

Crime and violence against women in its various forms is a violation of human rights, which deprives women of their ability to enjoy fundamental freedoms. It is a serious obstacle to equality between women and man. Scholars observe that violence against women remains hidden in the culture of silence as seen in Indian context. The causes and factors of violence against women include entranced unequal power relation between man and woman that fasten violence and acceptability, aggravated by the cultural and social norms, economic dependency, poverty and alcohol consumption etc. In India where the culprits are largely known to the victims, the social and economic 'cost' of reporting such as crimes are high. General economic dependence on their families and fear of social ostracization act as significant disincentive for a woman to report any kind of sexual violence or abuse. Therefore, the actual incidence of violence against women in India is probably much higher than the data suggested and because of this, most of the women are experiencing violence and living its consequences. There is need to break the silence and ensure that the violence against women is not just a women's issue, but primarily a political, social, economic and cultural issue that concerns men as well. While men represents the majority of perpetrators of violence against women because of their role models as father, husband, brother and sons, men and young boy should be the part of the solution and thus be involved in eliminating violence against women. If men felt involved, they should help promote changes in attitudes among other men.

3

Sexual Offences against Women: Specific Criminal Laws in India

Adrita Bhuyan

This is an attempt to examine the various legislations which are enshrined under the constitution for the protection and amelioration of women with special emphasis on the Indian Penal Code, 1860 (Herein after IPC). It has been observed statistically that crimes against women have been increasing despite the presence of various legislations related to sexual offences against women. The present endeavour put emphasis to understand the correlation between customary practices and prevalent laws in the country. Criminal laws were enacted to create a safe and secure stet of order according to the social contract theory. Thus, it is the prime responsibility of the state to protect women from any forms of sexual offences.

INTRODUCTION

The supreme law giver of the time Manu stipulated that:

'A woman must be dependent upon her father in childhood, upon her husband in youth and upon her sons in old age. She should never be free'.[1]

Indian women have ruled, concurred and proved their significance in the modern day world. Legislations in India in relation to women have been equalitarian since the very inception. In fact, India was one of the foremost countries to follow the principle of universal adult franchise which ensured that everyone irrespective of their gender, caste, colour, sex, etc had the right to vote. Recently, it is depicted that despite the presence of strict legislations, the situation of women in India has not improved in terms of crimes against women. It has been often stated that those who commit such crimes are psychologically sadistic persons exhibiting the tendency in rape forcibly committed by them.[2] Statistically, an idea about the magnitude of crime against women can be accessed from the All India figure for 5 years period starting from 2009 to 2013 published in the National Crime Record Bureau.[3] A total of 2,95,855 crimes against women was reported in 2013 as compared to 26,47,722 and head-wise incidents of crimes against women in 2009 to 2013.[4] Unfortunately, crime against women and their exploitation has multiplied in India many folds in recent years despite of a number of laws and public outcry to protect and safeguard their interest.[5] Laws came into existence in democratically free India for the protection and empowering women due to the prevalent orthodox legislations and patriarchal system of ancient India.

HISTORY OF WOMEN RELATED LEGISLATIONS

In ancient India, patriarchal system was highly prevalent due to which men dominated women.[6] Several inscriptions make references to the status of women in that they enjoyed the freedom to make liberal gifts to religious institutions like temples, Dharmasalas and other.[7] In the Vedic society women participated in religious ceremonies and tribal assemblies. There is no seclusion of women for domestic and social affairs. The hymns of the *Rig-Veda*, the *Adharva Veda* show that it was still customary for the widow to lay symbolically by the side of her husband's corpse on the funeral.[8] The position of women drastically changed in the Vedic period as women majorly lost their political rights. Marriage or domestic life became compulsory for women and unquestioning devotion to husband was their only duty. Along with dowry, the concept of Stridhan prevailed as well. At the time of her marriage, woman used to receive jewellery, land, etc., as gifts from her ancestral house and these were considered to be Stree Dhanam.[9] A Hindu woman, whether a maiden, a wife or a widow has never been denied the use of her property.[10] All law was originally customary law, and there was no statutory law in ancient India, for the simple reason that there was no parliament or legislature in those times[11]. The status of women from the Vedic period to the Post-Vedic has tremendously reduced. During the British era, women from upper-classes educated themselves and held important positions. After independence, women in India were empowered by laws that were enacted in the Constitution that ensured equality to the opposite gender. But, post independent India also encountered crimes against women in different forms despite progressive legislation due to staginess of social structure.

The central legislature in course of prevalent customary laws enacted a number of Acts supplementing the penal law of India.[12] Position of women in modern India has been considerably equal. Women have the right to receive education, inherit and own property and participate in public life. Several factors like women's education, reform movements, women's participation in politics and much social legislation are responsible for the changes in the country.

INDIAN CONSTITUTIONAL PROVISIONS

Throughout history and in many societies including India, gender inequality was an ingredient to male dominance. The principle of gender equality is enshrined in the Indian Constitution not only grants equality to women, but also empowers the state to adopt measures of positive discrimination in favour of women. The Constitution of India provided for reservation of seats in the local bodies of Panchayats and Municipalities for women.[13] Reserving 33 per cent seats in Parliament and State Legislature is significant. [14]

The Constitution prohibits discrimination against any citizen on grounds of religion, gender, race, caste, sex or place of birth, and guarantee equality of opportunity to all citizens in matters relating to employment.[15] The CEDAW defines 'discrimination against women' under Art.1 of the convention.[16] Ahead of venturing into legal punishments for crimes against women it is necessary to look into the constitutional provisions for women.[17] The law of the land awards adequate protection to protect the interest of women.[18] Essential provisions such as Art. 14,[19] Art. 15,[20] Art. 16,[21] Art. 19[22] and Art. 23[23] for the basis of basic structure. Article 39 (A) legal aid for women at state cost provided in the constitution has made elaborate arrangements to uplift the life and condition of women.[24] In spite of such constitutional guarantee and special laws enacted to give protection and ameliorate the status of women,[25] the real life scenario has not changed majorly. Though there are several reasons to this, but primarily the customary practices are to be blamed.

As per the report of the National Crime Record Bureau,[26] Sexual violence data, though, trends the other way. 16,528 were arrested for rape in 2011 which is double from 1991. Molestation and sexual harassment arrests from this cohort have also almost doubled, from 23,075 in 1992, the first year for which data is available, to 32,581 in 2011. Sexual offences constitute an all together different kind of crime which is the result of perverse mind. The perversity may result in rape or any other form of sexual offences. Those who commit such crimes are psychologically sadistic persons exhibiting the tendency in rape forcibly committed by them.[27] Thereby, reports suggest that offenders need to undergo therapy before rehabilitation into the society.

PENAL CODE LEGISLATIONS

As we observe the provisions in the Indian Penal Code, 1860, one of the most grievous acts of crime against women is rape that has been stated in Sec. 375 and 376 IPC,[28] wherein a rapist if proven, shall be punished with rigorous imprisonment of either description for a term which shall not be less than seven years, but which may extend to imprisonment for life, and shall also be liable to fine.' Under Sec. 375 IPC,[29] there are six main descriptions under which rape is considered to have been committed. The six conditions are when sexual intercourse is against her will, without her consent, with her consent but by putting her or another person of interest in fear of death or hurt, with consent when she mistaken with the identity of her husband, with her consent by reason of unsoundness or intoxicated mind and with or without consent when the girl is under 16 years of age. Rape convicted is punished death penalty according to recent amendments as per situation and nature.

There are certain exceptions in the IPC for rape wherein sexual intercourse by a man with his own wife, the wife not being under fifteen years of age, is not rape.[30] In the case of *Uday v. State of Karnataka*.[31] In this case was nearly the same wherein the prosecution, age 19 was raped against her consent which should be expressed or implied. India doesn't consider marital rape as a crime rather considers that if a woman is married, consent is implied to her husband. But there are provisions for cruelty under Hindu Marriage Act, 1955 as a ground for divorce.[32] In the case of *Deepak Gulati v. State of Haryana*,[33] paragraph 18 states that:

> "consent may be expressed or implied, coerced or misguided, obtained willingly or through deceit. There is a clear distinction between rape and consensual sex and in a case like this, the court must very carefully examine whether the accused had actually wanted to marry the victim, or had *mala fide* motives, and had made a false promise to this effect only to satisfy his lust, as the latter falls within the ambit of cheating or deception."

> *In Madan Gopal Kakkad v. Naval Dubey and another,*[34] the trial court acquitted the respondent for an offence under Sec. 376 IPC for having committed rape on girl child of 8 years of age. Aggrieved by the judgment of the trial court the State filed an appeal before the High Court challenging the order of acquittal. The High Court found the evidence of the victim satisfactory and convicted the respondent sentence to commensurate with gravity of offence.

Provisions related to Homicide for dowry, dowry deaths or their attempts are stated under Sec. 304-B IPC.[35] In the case of *Satvir Singh v. State of Punjab*,[36] the two-bench judgement by K T Thomas and S.N Variava the main question was whether the appellants can be convicted under Section 511 read with Section 304B IPC. There are certain essentials enlisted under Sec. 304B which includes death of a woman occurring otherwise than under normal circumstances, within 7 years of marriage and dowry demands immediately after marriage. When the above ingredients are fulfilled, the husband or his relative, who subjected her to such cruelty or harassment, can be presumed to be guilty of offence under Section 304B. Thereby, he will be liable under Sec. 304B and Sec. 511. In the case of *Kashmir Kaur v. State of Punjab*,[37] enlisted the main ingredients of the Sec. 304B of the IPC. Under this section, the prosecution will be liable only if the term 'dowry' is defined as per section 2 of the Dowry Prohibition Act, 1961. The Courts of India in several consecutive cases have enlisted the essential ingredients required for conviction under Sec. 304B. Other than that, Sec. 498-A that states punishment against husband or relative of husband of a woman subjecting her to cruelty which can be either mental or physical has also been mentioned in the IPC. This section is linked with the previous section of dowry as previous evidences have depicted cruel torture inflicted on the women by the husband or relative of husband to extract dowry by subjecting her to cruelty. If found guilty the accused shall be punished with imprisonment of either description for a term which may extend to three years, and shall also be liable to pay fine. In the case of *Prakash Kaur v. Harijinderpal Singh*,[38] the wife filed a petition for divorce on the ground of persistent demand made by her husband and her in-laws for money or equivalent demands, the High Court held that there was nothing wrong in the demand but Supreme Court considered this as an offence under dowry death. Sec. 354 defines molestation which states that an assault or criminal force to a women by either intention or knowing shall be punished with either imprisonment or fine. Section 509 states that insulting the modesty of women intending to show gestures or objects by intruding her privacy shall be punished with either imprisonment or fine. In the case of *M.M. Haries v. State of Kerala*,[39] paragraph 21 states that:

> "It is clear from a reading of Section 509 IPC that by introducing the said provision, legislature intended that any sort of aggression into a woman's modesty whether

by any word, deed or act should be deterred, as evident from the title to the section itself."

Thus, the acts which are conducted with the intention to insult the modesty of a woman which may not necessarily involve even any physical advances are also brought within the sweep of a separate provision viz., Section 509 IPC. After Court finds that the allegations revealed from the records constitute any offence or offences other than what are stated in the charge sheet, it will not be just and proper to quash the charge. This particular provision provides very stringent measure in regards to protection of the plea of the victim. Thus, there are several provisions in the IPC that protect the integrity of women and have laid down legal provisions that protect women from the crimes against the society. The formation of laws under IPC was mainly to mitigate the historical social structure which committed severe crimes against women in the society by subjecting her to cruelty and torture.

With emphasis on Sec. 313 of the IPC which is related to causing miscarriage of a women without her consent, to which Sec. 314 extends it to death caused to the woman with the intent to cause the miscarriage of a woman with child is liable under this section. There is a paucity of judgement in regards to Sec 313, thereby in the case of *Abdus Samad Sheikh v. State of Assam*,[40] the Gauhati High Court sentenced the accused appellant with simple imprisonment for 1 year under Sec 313 of the IPC. Under Sec 372 and Sec 373 wherein selling and buying minor for purpose of prostitution respectively has been stated. In the case of *Satya Pal Singh vs State Of M.P. and Ors*,[41] the accused was punished under Sections 372 and 373 of the IPC. In 1983 the IPC introduced changes in the offences relating to woman.[42] It was recommended by the 172nd Law Commission Report had for substantial change in the law with regard to rape by replacing the term 'rape with sexual assault'.[43] 'Rape' was substituted with *'Sexual Offences' by Act 43 of 1983*.[44] In the case of *Sakshi v Union of India & Ors*,[45] it was stated that sexual assault on any part of the body should be considered as rape. Further, the Criminal Law Amendment, 2013 brought significant changes into the IPC, IEA,[46] CrPC,[47] etc. Sec. 228A(1) stated that 'offence' shall be substituted in S. 376(A-E) and it made disclosure of rape victim's identity an offence.[48] S. 326A was inserted along with punishment under S. 326B for acid attack with a punishment which may extend to imprisonment for life and fine. Even after the 2013 reform, marital rape is not a crime in India. However, it is considered a form of prosecutable domestic violence under different sections of IPC, such as Section 498 (A) as well as the Articles of DVA, 2005. Sec. 498A was added with a view to punish husband and his relatives who harass or torture the wife to coerce her or her relatives to satisfy unlawful demands of dowry like in the case *Rita v. Brij Kishore*.[49]

Also, in the case of *Rishi Kumar v. State of Haryana*,[50] the allegations against the husband were that he abused and beat his wife, forced her to have a common kitchen with a harijan family, accused her of adultery and pressurized her for abortion against her will and such acts amounted to wilful conduct of cruelty towards her wife which made the husband liable under Sec. 498A of the IPC. Sec. 509 states that "whosoever intends to insult the modesty of any woman, utters any words, makes any sound or gesture, or exhibits any object, intending that such word or sounds shall be heard, or that such gesture or object shall be seen, by such woman, or intrudes upon the privacy of such woman". If a person is convicted got the above, he shall be punished with simple imprisonment for a term which may extend to three years and also with fine.[51] The above sections mainly cover all the protection that is awarded to women in India for their protection and empowerment. The sections have been placed, while their implementation is a matter of concern for the country. The rate of crimes against women in the country has been ever increasing even in the presence of legal reforms.

An idea about the magnitude of the crime against women can be had from the All India figures for 9 years from 2001 to 2009 published in the National Crime Record Bureau [52] . Under Sec 354 of the IPC that states punishment on 'Assault or criminal force to woman with intent to outrage her modesty' the assigned punishment is with either imprisonment of for a term which may extend to two years, or with fine, or with both.[53] State amendments such as Andhra Pradesh, Chhattisgarh and Madhya Pradesh have disparate punishment for the same offence. In the state of Andhra Pradesh, the culprits are awarded with a punishment with imprisonment of either description for a term which shall not be less than five years but which may extent to seven years and shall also be liable to fine.[54] Chhattisgarh provided a wide meaning to the section that a relative, guardian or teacher or a person in a position of trust or authority towards the person assaulted shall be punishable with imprisonment of either description for a term which shall not be less than two years but which may extended to seven years and shall be liable to fine.[55] Madhya Pradesh stated in regards to action of abetment or conspiracy of a person towards assaulting a women intending to outrage or knowing assault the modesty of a woman by disrobing or compel her to be naked on any public place, shall be punished with imprisonment or either description for a term which shall not be less than one year but which may extend to ten years and shall also be liable to pay fine.[56]

As per section 354A 'sexual harassment and punishment for sexual harassment' if convicted shall be punished with rigorous imprisonment for a term which may extend to three years, or with fine, or with both. For the next clause that is (iv) under the same sub-sections shall be punished with imprisonment of either description for a term which may extend to one year, or with fine, or with both. In the case of *T Manikadan v. The State (Govt of NCT of Delhi),*[57] before the High Court, convict was punished for an offence under Sections 354/354A IPC and was directed to undergo simple imprisonment for a period of one year. Under section 354B, assault or use of criminal force to woman with intent to disrobe' wherein it states that if convicted then shall be punished with imprisonment of either description for a term not less than three years but which may extend to seven years, and shall also be liable to fine. Under section 354C 'Voyeurism' states that if convicted then shall be punished on first conviction with imprisonment of either description for a term which shall not be less than one year, but which may extend to three years, and shall also be liable to fine, and be punished on a second or subsequent conviction, with imprisonment of either description for a term which shall not be less than three years, but which may extend to seven years, and shall also be liable to fine.[58] The concept of 'private act' has also been explained under this section.[59] There are certain situations when a victim might consent the capturing of the images of their 'private parts' but might not accept the concept of dissemination of the images. Such dissemination shall be considered an offence under this section.[60] Section 354D 'stalking',[61] emerged due to increasing crime rates. It states if convicted then the person shall be punished on first conviction with imprisonment of either description for a term which may extend to three years, and also be liable to fine. In the second conviction, punishment with imprisonment of either description for a term which may extend to five years, and shall also be liable to fine as Sec. 354D(2). There are certain exceptions such as the person accused of stalking was entrusted with the duty of preventing or detecting crime by the State or by law or to comply with any condition or requirement imposed by any person under any law; or under reasonable and justified conditions.

In *State of Kerala v. Hamsa*,[62] the term 'modesty' by the legislature under Sec 354 and 509 of the Indian Penal Code was for the protection of an attribute which is peculiar to woman or virtues attached to women. Modesty is the attribute of female sex and she possesses it irrespective of her age.

In most cases, the facts of the case decide the offence to be awarded. In the case, *State of Karnataka v. Khaleel*,[63] stated as "the parents reached the sugarcane field when accused was in process of attempting molestation and immediately he ran away from the place. There was no evidence in support of allegation of rape and accused was acquitted of charge u/s 376 but he was held liable for conviction under Sec. 354/ 511 IPC. Similarly, In the case *Nuna v. Emperor*,[64] states "The accused took off a girl's clothes, threw her on the ground and then sat down beside her. He said nothing to her nor did he do anything more. It is held that the accused committed an offence under Sec. 354 IPC and was not guilty of an attempt to commit rape." The court in *Keshab Padhan v. State of Orissa*,[65] states "the test of outrage of modesty is whether a reasonable man will think that the act of the offender was intended to or was known to be likely to outrage the modesty of the woman." The court in *Shokut v State of Rajasthan*,[66] states, " the accused took the prosecution nurse for the purpose of attending a patient but on way he tried to molest her and beat her also. The accused was held guilty u/s 354/366 IPC as he by deceitful means had taken the prosecution from her house and had then outraged her modesty." In *Bishewhwar Murmu v. State of Jharkhand*, [67] states that accused caught hold hand of informant/victim and when one of the prosecution witnesses came there hearing alarm of victim. The accused was convicted under section 354 of the IPC rather than Sec. 376/511 of the IPC.

ANALYSIS

While we study the ingredients and nature of each provision to sexual offences related to women, the violation of legal provisions of the IPC, results in crimes against women. There have been several instances wherein courts have ruled in favour of the women. The legislations are more towards the protection of women in India. Despite the alarming increase in crimes against men in the recent times, there have been hardly any provisions for crimes against men.

The legislations of the IPC were initially introduced in order to create a fair environment for women, due to the long history of pending cases of crimes against women. Even recent instances such as the Nirbhaya case, which gave rise to the Criminal Law Amendment Act, 2013 depicted that our women are far from safe. Based on the recommendations which were provided by the Justice Verma Committee in relation to anti-rape ordinance was enacted and signed by the then President. Following which the Amendment Bill, 2013 was passed. With the further introduction of Criminal Law Amendment, 2013 there were significant amendments to the IPC, CrPC, IEA and the Protection of Children from Sexual Offences Act, 2012 which came into force on 3rd February, 2013 with insertion of some specific provisions such as Sec. 326A. Sec. 326B, Amendment of Sec. 354 with further insertion of sections 354, 354A. 354B, 354c and Sec. 354D, substitution of new sections for sections 375,376, 376A, 376B, 376C and 376D. Despite the introduction of the Criminal Law Amendment, 2013 the rates of crimes against women have not decreased. While we emphasize that more strict legislations should be enforced, we also observe the stricter legislations do no ensure that crime rates against women will subsequently decrease.

Though it has been repeatedly stated that stated punishments awarded for the crimes are not sufficient, we need to understand that in several case the offenders despite being punished with rigorous punishments such as long terms of imprisonments or fine or even life imprisonment, do not exempt themselves from committing more crimes against women either after their release or during their stay in the jail. Observations state that the overall mentality, customary practices and the age old traditions have resulted in such repeated instances. Since centuries women have been always subjected as the subordinate sex in the patriarchal system. Thereby, introduction of new legislation will not limit or reduce the existing attitude or mental personality of the society about women. Thus, that laws in India have several provisions which allow legal remedy to both the parties in the matter. Even after declaring a particular order, there are certain review petitions which are filed to be exempt from the awarded punishment. Though it is justified for them to exercise the power conferred by law, but the process keeps elongating the justice delivery system. Thereby, this ensures that most offenders are not scared of the punishments or the legislations drafted for the protection of women because they believe that most victims will not voluntarily enter into the long justice delivery system. Criminal offences are against the State. The life of the victim changes its course after the execution of the offence due to the mental stress that the victim goes through. Courts should make attempts at simplifying the process of investigation and litigation such that the victim does not have to go through a similar mental stress repeatedly.

CONCLUSION

Thus, it is concluded that IPC laid down strong influential laws for the protection of women in the society, however, there applicability has to be enforced in order to have a fair and free society. It can be rightly stated that stringent legislations results in increase of court proceedings due to which culprits are not apprehensive of the punishments awarded under the IPC, thereby increasing crime rates.

END NOTES

1. Vinay Sharma, *Dowry Death: Legal Provisions and Judicial Interpretation*, 14-18, Deep and Deep Publications (2007)
2. T.K Gopal alias *Gopi v. State of Karanataka*, 2000 3 Supreme 706 (India)
3. K D Gaur, *Criminal Law: Cases and Materials*,700-706, LexisNexis, 8th edition (2015)
4. *Ibid.*
5. K.D.Gaur, Commentry on the Indian Penal Code, 1162-1164, Universal Law Publishing Co., 2nd Edition (2013)
6. S.A. Rehman, *The Beauty of India: Andhra Pradesh*, 224, Reference Press, New Delhi (2005)
7. *Ibid.*
8. *Ibid.*
9. *Ibid.*
10. Women property rights: a comparative study of Hindu, Christian and Muslim, Shodhagana, Jawaharlal Nehru University, Chapter 4. As for reference < https://sg.inflibnet.ac.in/bitstream/10603/201578/8/08_chapter%204.pdf>
11. Justice Markandey Katju, Ancient Indian Jurisprudence Judge, Supreme Court of India Speech delivered on 27.11.2010 at Banaras Hindu University, Varanas, As for reference https://www.bhu.ac.in/mmak/resent_article/JusticeKatjusLec.pdf
12. The Indian Penal Code, No. 45 of 1860,INDIA CODE, (1961).
13. Indian Constitution, added part IX and IXA, The Constitution (Seventy third Amendment) Act, 1993 and The Constitution (Seventy Fourth Amendment) Act, 1993.
14. *Women's Reservation Bill: All you need to know about the bill which will bring 33 percent reservation for women in Lok Sabha*, India Today, Mar. 7, 2020, https://www.indiatoday.in/education-today/gk-current-affairs/story/women-s-reservation-bill-all-you-need-to-know-about-the-bill-which-is-yet-to-be-passed-in-lok-sabha-1653451-2020-03-07

15. Priti Diliprao Pohekar *Constitutional And Legal Provisions For Women In India*, IJHAMS.L.J, 81,81-86, (2015).
16. *Article I, Convention on the Elimination of All Forms of Discrimination against Women New York, 18 December 1979*
17. Kamal Kumar Pandey & Rishi Kant, *Legal Provisions in IPC and C.r.P.C for Women*, OLR, Odisha Review P. 2-5. (2011)
18. *Ibid.*
19. Indian Constitution. art. 14
20. ibid
21. ibid
22. ibid
23. ibid
24. *Ibid*
25. *Ibid*
26. Report of Committee on the Amendments to Criminal Law, 2013, As for reference https://www.prsindia.org/uploads/media/Justice%20verma%20committee/js%20verma%20committe%20report.pdf
27. T.K Gopal alias Gopi v. State of Karanataka,3 Supreme 706 (SC), 2000, (India)
28. S. 376 : Punishment for Rape, IPC, 1860
29. S. 375 : Raoe, IPC, 1860
30. Ibid
31. AIR 2003 SC 1639 (India)
32. Section 13, Hindu Marriage Act, 1955
33. AIR 2013 SC 2071 (India)
34. AIR (1992) 3 SCC 204 (India)
35. S. 304B: Dowry Death, IPC, 1860
36. AIR 2001 SC 2828 (India)
37. AIR 2013 SC 1039 (India)
38. AIR 1999 Raj 46 (India)
39. MANU/KE/0744/2005
40. Cri Appeal 140 of 2008, GHC, Date of judgment 14th September, 2017. As for reference http://ghconline.nic.in/Judgment/CrlA1402008.pdf
41. MANU/SC/1119/2015MANU/SC/1119/2015

42. Prof. K.N. Chandrasekharan Pillai & Shabistan Aquil, Essays on the Indian Penal Code, The Indian Law Institute, (2008)
43. RC Jiloha, From *rape to sexual assault: Legal provisions and mental health implications*, 9-18, (2015).
44. *Ibid.*
45. (2004) 5 SCC 518 (India)
46. Indian Evidence Act, 1872
47. The Code of Criminal Procedure, 1972
48. Inserted by Act 43 of 1983, Sec. 2.IPC
49. AIR 1984 Del 291
50. Criminal Appeal No. 335-B of 1985
51. Universal's *Criminal Manual*, Lexis Nexis P. 524-598-C, (2017)
52. Crimes in India, 2009, National Crime Record Bureau, p. 83 (India)
53. *Ibid*
54. *Andhra Pradesh Act 6 of 1991*
55. *Chhattisgarh Act 25 of 2015, section 3 of the act.*[1]
56. The Madhya Pradesh Act 14 of 2004, sec. 3 of the aforementioned act
57. CRL.REV.P. 404/2016 & & Crl.M.B. 1114/2016
58. Sec. 354 (C), Indian Penal Code, 1860
59. Explanation 1, Sec. 354 (C), Indian Penal Code, 1860
60. Explanation 2, Sec. 354 (C), Indian Penal Code, 1860
61. headline
62. (1988) 3 Cri 161
63. 2004 CrLJ 10
64. 15 IC 309 : 13 CrLJ 469
65. 1976 Cut LR (Cr) 236
66. (2002) CrLJ 364 (Raj)
67. 2004 CrLJ 326

4

Women's Journey towards Criminality

Shubhank Gour

INTRODUCTION

We were living in a society where only men were dominating, that can be also called as patriarchy. Since the beginning of the justice system, the experiences of women either have been reduced to cursory glance or have been completely absent. Gender injustice had prevailed in every aspect of the society. The unique experiences of women had historically been ignored at every turn for victims, for offenders, and even for women who have worked within its walls. But actually women are the founding stone of the family in particular and society in general. In India, especially, the woman, be it the mother, the daughter, or the wife, is seen as the preserver of social norms, morality, customs, traditions and family cohesiveness. The woman is supposed to be submissive, passive, compassionate and ready to compromise in order to maintain the family. As pointed out by Kate Millet, women are relegated to an inferior status in the society. Despite adequate provisions under various laws, they have been discriminated on the ground of sex for centuries. Deprivation of women of their basic human rights and equal status with men is a historical phenomenon which dominates the life of the communities around the world. French writer Simone de Beavoir observed that in a patriarchal society, women is looked by men as a sex object and no more. They are differentiated with reference to men as inferior with socio-economic and cultural prohibitions and restrictions imposed on them which are irrational and unreasonable and result of gender inequality. Irrespective of such facts that women make up a majority of the victims for certain types of crimes such as rape, sexual assault, criminal intimidation, harassment, etc. So many feminist movements lead so many changes in this society that may be helpful to bring back the glory of the women which was hidden or was not provided to them. But with the evolution of many rights to the women there is another face of the women nature also evolves that is the pink collar crime.

The social and cultural development of the modern era has led to the emergence of the feminist legal concern for law which has assumed considerable importance in the recent years. The study of women and crime has seen incredible advances throughout the 20th and 21st century. Prior to this era the women would be imagined only as a victim or weaker section of the society, but with the beginning of this era criminology scholars began to think differently about women and offending. But with the development of the feminist movement, by getting many rights the criminal intension in the minds of the women were also developed. As we can say that women and crime can be classified as women as a victim and as an offender.

WOMEN AS A VICTIM

In among everywhere in the whole world the condition of women is quite similar in old centuries. Somewhere the society is patriarchal (male dominating) or somewhere social injustice, skepticism and masculine legal approach which adversely affect women's integration in total development. In our country the condition of women is not good. So many customs like *Sati* systems (burning widow women with the burial of her husband); *pardah pratha* was there, women used to kept inside the house only no right to move out freely, and many more. This all clearly shows the worse condition of women prevailing in the society in the past. Therefore due to various efforts various feminist movement the concern against sex based discrimination and protection of rights of women finds expressions in various United Nations Conventions and Resolutions. Article 8 of the U.N. Charter provides that, 'U.N. shall place no restrictions on the eligibility of men and women to participated in any capacity under conditions of equality and its principal and subsidiary organs.' Universal Declaration of Human Rights (1948) which set out general norms of non-discrimination made sex one of the impermissible grounds of discrimination and laid down provision for equal protection of women. This was subsequently reiterated in Article 2 (1), 3, and 26 of the International Covenant on Civil and political Right, 1966 and Article 2(2) and 3 of the International Covenant on the Economic, Social, and Cultural Rights, 1966. The International Labor Organization (ILO) adopted the principle of equal remuneration for work of equal value for men and women as a policy resolution in 1951. Similarly in India in order to eliminate the gender discrimination, there are several efforts.

Followings are the few constitutional provisions which seek to implement the objective of gender justice in society as under: (legislative approach): right to equality before law and equal protections of the laws (Article 14), prohibition of discrimination on the ground of sex {Article 15(1)}, state can make special provisions for promoting and safeguarding the interest of women and children {article 15(3)}, affirmative action or reservation for women (Article 16), reservation of seats for women In Panchayat and Local bodies and Municipalities (73rd ad 74th constitutional amendments,1992), just and human conditions of work and maternity benefit for Women (Article 42), state to endeavour to ensure living wages etc. for workers including women (Article 43), equal pay for equal work for both men and women {article 39(d)} and one of the fundamental duties of every citizen on India to denounce all practices which are derogatory to the dignity of women { Article 51-A(e)}. Besides these provisions of the constitution some other legislative measures protecting women against gender discrimination is: Child Marriage Restraint Act, 1978, The Commission of Sati (prevention) Act,1987, Indecent Representation of Women (prohibition)Act,1986, Immoral Traffic (prevention) Act,1956, Dowry Prohibition Act,1961, Equal Remuneration Act, 1976, The Medical Termination of Pregnancy Act,1971, Maternity Benefit act,1961, Pre-natal Diagnostic Techniques Act,1974, Protection of Women from Sexual Harassment at Workplace Act 2013, Anti-Rape Criminal (amendment) of IPC...in 2013 and 2018 and National Commission For Women Act,1990. These legislative approach apart, there are various judicial approach that can be understand through various case laws. In the case of *State of Punjab V. Ramdev* AIR 2004 SC1290, Supreme Court expresses concern for the lack of gender sensibility: "An unmerited acquittal of rapist does no good to the society. If the prosecution has succeeded in making out a convincing case for recording a finding as to the accused being guilty, the court should not lean in favor of acquittal by giving weight to irrelevant and insignificant circumstances or by resorting to technicalities or by assuming doubt and giving benefits thereof where none reasonably exists. A doubt has to be reasonable doubt and not an excise for finding in favor of acquittal. An unmerited acquittal encourages and evolves in the society being on the prowl for easy prey, more so when victim of rape are helpless females or minor children."

Adopting a pro-feminist approach, the Supreme Court in *Jugendra Singh V. State of U.P.* AIR 2012 SC 2254, observed: "The rape and attempt to rape in a crime not against an individual but a crime which destroys the basis equilibrium of the social atmosphere. The consequential death is more horrendous. It is to be set in mind that offences against body of a woman lower her dignity and mars her reputation. It is said that one's physical frame is his/her temple. No one has any right of encroachment. An attempt for the momentary pleasure of the accused has caused the death of a child and had a devastating effect on her family and in the ultimately eventuate on the collective society at large. When a family suffers in such a manner, the society as a whole is compelled to suffer as it creates an incurable dent in the fabric of the social milieu. The cry has to be answered and respected and that is what exactly the High Court has done by converting the decision of acquittal of that conviction imposed as per law."

WOMEN AS AN OFFENDER

In the recent decades, women's participation in every field of development has increased considerably in most of the countries and is converging towards the participation rate of men. Though on a lesser scale, a similar movement toward gender convergence seems to be occurring in the criminal world, though many more men than women still engage in criminal activity. Technological progress and social norms have freed women from the home, increasing their participation in almost every field including crime also. With crime no longer just men's business, it is important to investigate female criminal behavior to determine whether the policy prescriptions to reduce crime should differ for women.

FEMALE OFFENDING IN INDIA

Male and female offenders are not treated equally in India. Judges often go beyond the law and apply social and cultural biases in determining whether a female suspect is liable, and in sentencing her if convicted. It ultimately argues that there is a dire need for rectifying this biases outlook, to take into account the social realities of a female offender, and judge her accordingly. The Supreme Court of India has opined that, though gender is not a mitigating factor in many countries of the world, however, as far as the Indian Judiciary is concerned, gender is relevant circumstance taken into consideration while deciding a quantum of the sentenced to be given to a female criminal. Insofar as the sentencing of convicted female offenders is concerned, there is a complex dilemma to be considered. On the one hand, in terms of the wide discretionary powers given to judges for sentencing of offenders, if the judiciary takes into account certain mitigating factors from the female offender's life, then there is a high possibility that it is portraying a misogynistic mentality which is based on outdated and archaic assumptions about a women in that situation, and about the 'weaker' sex in general. This is evident from the cases of *Satni Bai V. State of Madhya Pradesh (Now Chhattisgarh)* and *Lichhamadevi V. State of Rajasthan.* In the former, the accused-appellant was found standing near the dead body of her son with a bloodstained axe in her hand. The court observed that any mother's normal reaction would be to go hysterical and clutch the body of her son. Therefore, the unusual reaction of the appellant was used as a ground to determine her involvement in the crime, and she was thus convicted. In the latter case, the accused-appellant was convicted for the murder of her daughter-in-law, because she had harassed the deceased for dowry, had an 'overbearing', 'barbaric' attitude, and was the 'master of the house'. On this basis the court held her guilty. Therefore, we see that a court's discretionary sentencing power can at times become discriminatory. In such situations, the certainty of the criminal law is destroyed, as there is no uniformity in sentencing patterns across cases. The fact that sometimes judges try to find some sort of relation between biological identity and criminality also plays a minor role here. In the case of *Smt. Paniben V. State of Gujarat,* where a woman burned her daughter-in-law alive by throwing kerosene on her and lighting it, the court spoke about her saying that even the mother in her didn't prevent her from committing this act, that it was quite unfortunate that a female should kill another female in this manner.

WHY DO WOMEN COMMIT CRIMES?

Thinkers entered the discussion on criminal behavior with a pioneering 1968 study that looks at criminals as rational actors who decide to commit a crime if the expected benefit are higher than the expected constant other words, when all the other variables are held constant, a change in the incentives to engage in criminal activities leads to increase (or decrease) in the number of crime committed. The decision to commit crime depends upon many reasons are as: less probability of being caught, probable length and severity of the sentence if the perpetrator is caught; Unexpected behavior of women as an offender in the eye of society and the disutility of going to jail, less working opportunities and earning measures and risk aversion, also of biological reason as Pollak elucidated the influence of hormonal changes over menstruation, pregnancy and menopausal stage. He stated that in the pregnancy and menopausal phase, the psychological characteristics such as emotional changes of moods, abnormal craving and impulses and temporary impairment of consciousness point in the direction of criminal causation. There are other reasons. Women who are not passive and content with their traditional roles as mothers and wives are maladjusted. Maladjusted women refuse or fails to internalize the 'Values of associated' with the role in the society. Women convicts display emotional instability, insecurity, rejection and frustration. They would have encounter harsh living conditions, disappointments in love and a large number of unfortunate experiences which generally made it difficult for them to face realities of life. Stress is higher for women on average than men, primarily due to blocked opportunities, and the conflicting message of motherhood versus work. Women bottle up their feelings until it finally explodes in lethal violence. Therefore psychological viewpoint may also leads a woman to indulge into a crime like aggression, assault and many more. There are some social factors leads to a woman turning a criminal. Woman in spite of so much development and awareness faces inequalities in every face of life. Equality for woman yet not practiced nowadays. Due to inequalities, women miss most of the opportunities in life which in turn affect her financial independence and thus her economic status is lowered. Therefore it is not wrong to say that due to this social suppression to the life of women may lead a woman towards the commission of crime.

WHICH CRIMES DO WOMEN COMMITS?

Women offender is increasing in all around the world. In the US, both men and women engage mostly in crime against property, including burglary, theft, car theft and white collar crime. Property crimes represent almost 70% of the total crimes for women and around 50% for men who are in prison. The share of drug crimes and violent crimes is almost twice as high among men as among women. In England and Wales, crimes against the person and drug offences are the most common crimes for both men and women. Gender gaps in the types of crime committed by people who have been imprisoned for their crimes are greatest for drug offences (30% of the crime committed by women and 17% of the crime committed by men), theft and handling stolen gods (14% for women and 5% for men), fraud and forgery (8% women and 3% men), sexual offences (2% for women and 17% for men). In Italy, as in England and Wales, drug offence, theft and handling stolen goods are the most common crimes for all people imprisoned for a crime. Women tend to commit more theft (38% of the crime committed by women and 23% of the crime committed by the men) and fraud (13% for the women and 6% for the men), while men commit more robberies (8% for men and 4% for women) and violence against persons (18% for men and 10% for women). Even in India,(Government of India, 2011) gives the statistical representation of female criminality in India. The crime rate within a decade in India is in increasing trends and female criminalities getting extended from minor crime to heinous crimes. Total crimes committed by females increased from 144608 to 193555 that is the percent increase of crime committed by female increase from 5.4% in 2001 to 6.2% in 2011. Female committing heinous crime like murder is at rise from 4.6% to 6.3% in 2011. And attempt to commit murder by female has increased from 2.6% to 4.2% in a decade and so on till date. The rate is increasing day by day.

FEMALE CRIMINALITY IN INDIA

In India also the social environment contributes a lot to the making of women criminals. The society of India was a patriarchal society, where the women were only considered as an object used to keep inside the walls of a house, to take care of children and to cook food. She does not have any right to move freely out of the house and considered only as an object of exploitation that leads to the increase of criminality in India. According to Psychologist 'Anchal Bhagat', the female offenders have lost faith in social system. Women fate is sealed and they face deprivation instead of constitutional rights and privileges. Discrimination within society exists from birth till last breath in most parts in India, in her work, had mentioned one such very famous example about a victim turned victimizer, Phoolan Devi. Her story as a victimizer starts with failing to give her justice. Phoolan Devi denied of justice had turned notorious bandit queen who later became politician. However, in her short struggle-full life she had gained lot of enemies and she was murdered. Stating an example like this Bhagat concludes that the compelling factors such as want of economic independence, recognition in society and to earn respectable position in the society is what probably forces women like Phoolan Devi to resort to extreme steps of taking law in their hands. Like that there were many incidents in the past which shows a status of criminality among women in India. The principle of judicial chivalry is clearly depicted in those cases where the court defends a woman in order to pronounce a judgement of acquittal. According to this principle, women are treated as less responsible for their action, therefore less culpable. Thus, women are treated as being less criminally dangerous than men and posing a lesser threat to society. Daly suggests that the emphasis of chivalry is not so much on the female offender herself, but on the husband and children of the offender. This is clearly evident in the case *Shantabai and ors V State of Maharashtra,* where the court went to great lengths to hold that there was no illicit relation between the prime accused and the deceased. It did so by noting that she was happily married and living with her husband and children. Therefore, what emerges is that the focus is not on the woman, but on the need to preserve the fabric of society.

CONCLUSION AND SUGGESTIONS

Many revolutions bring so many changes in the lifestyle of women. Now women are independent in almost each sphere of her life but with this positive change in the condition of women their bring the existence of a negative change i.e., the attitude towards the crime. The women now started indulging in criminal activities also which must be ignored in recent past but nowadays these issues came in front of us. The statistical data from everywhere is coming to us which clearly shows the women participation in crime. Many law agencies and investigation agencies are now keeping their eyes on the criminal action of women attentively and very effectively. Nowadays women are not an only subject of harassment and oppression but now she came out from this mentality and got so many rights for her upliftment in the society. But somewhere it could be seen in past her attitude towards crime been ignored by our law and order. A lenient treatment should be given to her may leads her towards crime therefore it must be necessary that we must come out of such a mentality that crime can only be done by a men and no women can commit any crime and various measures should be taken to kept women out and away from such a criminal world. We can follow the following measures:

Preventive measures

It is said that prevention is better than cure and having said that, in case of crime and its prevention that is a humongous task. Crime prevention among the female is a bigger challenge because it is difficult to recognize the vulnerable areas and people especially women. Generally awareness of the role of woman in a society, her rights and laws for them should be briefed to the uneducated women. Legal awareness and awareness about illegal activities and to report or keep themselves away from illegal activities should be provided by social services/adult educations unit. Sex education plays an important role wherein the women indulge in crime following lack of awareness regarding sex-rackets and flesh trade. And also need to be informed about the harsh laws against being a part of such crime. Proper counseling and education should be provided to at most each level of the society i.e. from higher to the very low level of the society, and raise people awareness towards it.

Corrective measures

Female criminals who are serving their term in the prison due to crime committed by them or in collaboration with others companions or offenders, should be given a chance to rectify or correct their ways so that when they finish their term of imprisonment and come out of the prison, they should be a lady with no criminal attributes, well informed and more aware, which would enable her to stay away from the crime and others criminals. In prison they should be given training of cooking, tailoring, painting, gardening, etc. so that she can become independent and earn her livelihood when she came out from jail.

Rehabilitative and supportive measures

A female criminal should be given chance to fulfill her parental responsibilities. Attention should be paid on providing female prisoner with proper medical aid and even on rehabilitation. In case if a female prisoner is suffering from any illness than she should be given proper medical facilities and proper aid. Proper access to their family and to consult legal advisor should be given to her with a due procedure is to be followed before meeting. It should be always kept in mind that a women offender who commits less severe nature offence must be kept away from such women who are indulging in more severe nature offence and must not meet each other, because it may leads the change of psychology of that woman same as the others.

Others measures

Equal rights and supports not only be given only in a paper work, but it must be properly implemented and proper watching should be there in order to find out whether, women are using that right as a shield of as a sword. Sometimes we give a right in order to protect someone but the others used to take unnecessary advantage of it that must be carefully examined.

5

Crime and Torture against Women

Sarthak Arora

"While women weep, as they do now, I'll fight; while children go hungry, as they do now I'll fight; while there is a poor lost girl upon the streets, while there remains one dark soul without the light of God, I'll fight, I'll fight to the very end!"

-William Booth

INTRODUCTION

Ordinarily, everyone is battling for their rights. Somebody is moving towards court for property matters, somebody is moving towards court for senseless family disputes, however, has anybody at any point given an idea to the state of those individuals who are confronting mental torcher pretty much consistently by carrying on with a detached life far from the general public. It is about those women detainees who are living far from their family and confronting mental and physical badgering, by the society as well as even by the jail authorities. The term 'violence against women' has been utilized to depict a wide scope of acts, including murder, assault and rape, physical attack, psychological mistreatment, battering, stalking, prostitution, genital mutilation, lewd behavior, and pornography. There is little agreement in the still developing field on precisely how to define violence against women. The significant dispute concerns whether to carefully define the word 'violence' or to think about the expression 'violence against women' all the more comprehensively as forceful practices that adversely and disproportionately influence women. Truly, women have been prohibited from political life and decision-making processes. Women's campaigns for participation in the public and political field go back to the nineteenth and twentieth centuries and proceed with today.

India, a country which had Mahatma Gandhi as its good example of integrity turned out to be so extraordinarily savage and degenerate that the women can never again be safe within their bodies. Gandhi who vanquished the whites to spare the browns by depending on peacefulness is considered as the father of the nation, however, his values are being betrayed so effectively that a woman is raped every twenty minutes [1] in the world's largest democracy and even children of five years are exposed to rape. [2] Financial experts foresee that the future has a place with India as the nation is fixated on comprehensive development and the men with status and power, however, the women who bring forth these men live in dread of segregation and sexual violence.

As Hon'ble Justice Krishna Iyer said in Sunil Batra case[3] "convicts are not by mere reason of the conviction denuded of all the fundamental rights which they otherwise possess." UDHR guideline, 1948 also says that: "no one shall be subject to crimes and torture or cruel, inhuman or degrading treatment of punishment."

CUSTODIAL CRIMES AND TORTURE AGAINST WOMEN

Article 21 of the Constitution ensures the right of personal liberty and thereby prohibits any inhuman, cruel or degrading treatment to any person. In any case, the fact of the matter is actually inverse as prisoners' major rights are encroached at every second. Indeed, even the prisoners do have some human rights. They additionally have a right to be treated as a 'human'. On the off chance that a woman perpetrates any wrongdoing, it doesn't imply that by carrying out a wrongdoing, she stops to be a human being and she can be denied of those parts of life which establishes human dignity. The state is under a commitment for securing the human rights of the prisoners too.

Women, who more often than not have ensured protected lives. From childhood they are ensured under the shelter of their father and after marriage under the haven of their spouses. However, when those women come in conflict with law and imprisoned, it becomes impossible for them to adapt to the prison conditions. Prison secludes the women from their family and companions. What's more, the greater part of the occasions even their family and companions dismiss them, which bring sadness, blame, crimes and torture on them. Generally, the greater part of the prison detainees are males, and the prison condition is in this way formed by the needs of males and don't take into account the uncommon needs of women prisoners. The gender discrimination and disadvantage gets worse amid imprisonment, which is additionally intensified upon their discharge from prison. Women in prison experience the ill effects of double disadvantage. Women prisoners every now and then become the victims of physical and sexual abuse by the jail authority themselves. On occasion, male staff does not dither to do frisk search on female prisoners. There are occurrences when prison staff have embraced and upheld bullying and verbal abuse of women prisoners, in the event that they don't listen to them.

The Indian Supreme Court has been dynamic in reacting to human right violations in Indian jails and has, simultaneously, perceived various privileges of detainees by interpreting Articles 21, 19, 22, 12, 17 and 19A of the Constitution in a positive and sympathetic way. In a landmark judgment of *Sheela Barsey v. State of Maharashtra* [4], the Hon'ble court has given certain guidelines such as: "four or five lock ups should be selected reasonably good localities where only female prisoners should be kept which should be guided by female suspects only. Interrogation of female suspects should be in front of female constables only".

Furthermore, the topic of cruelty to detainees is managed, by the Prisons Act, 1894. The Prisoners Act, 1900 arrangements with specific guidelines of jail to be trailed by Jail Authorities. Section 46 of Criminal Procedure Code, 1971 also provides with a provision for women prisoners, which clearly states that: "no women shall be arrested after sunset and before sunrise."

The All India Committee on Jail Reforms (1980-1981), the Supreme Court of India and the Committee of Empowerment of Women (2001-2002) have all featured the requirement for a far-reaching modification of the jail laws yet the pace of any change has been baffling. The Supreme Court of India has anyway extended the skylines of prisoner's rights jurisprudence through a progression of judgments. However, despite such a large number of guidelines by judiciary, the state of women prisoners is deteriorating step by step. It is great said 'women's chains have been forged by men, not by anatomy.'[5] Custodial horror is a day by day event for women prisoners in India. All things considered, what would women be able to do when their 'caretakers' turned into their violators? The inquiry is exceptionally scary and unnerving however this is really happening to women in India. There have been multitudinous situations where 'men-in-khaki,' have been found insulting the women prisoners' modesty, inside and as well as even outside the jails. Women prisoners in India are raped as well as they are even killed mercilessly by policemen.

The territory of Maharashtra has enrolled the most noteworthy number of custodial deaths for example, 116, trailed by Uttar Pradesh (255). As indicated by the National Human Rights Commission, there are 2118 instances of custodial deaths over the nation, all of which have been submitted by policemen, since October 1991. A couple of women who served jail terms have asserted crimes and torture and cruel treatment inside the detainment facilities crosswise over Tamil Nadu. Three remand women prisoners, addressed the media at a gathering sorted out by the campaign against custodial equity and annulment of crimes and torture of the Society for Integrated Rural Development and said that they were stripped exposed and abused verbally and physically and they were not given the fundamental necessities.[6] A comparable occurrence from Khetri Jail, Rajasthan happened, where two guards ransomed a lady and kept her for seven days. [7]

Crimes and torture against women in reformatory care is considered as an especially serious infringement of human rights with uplifted obligation from the state for the person in its authority. In U.S., the law-making body has instituted a particular enactment named as The Prison Rape Elimination Act, 2001 for the welfare of women prisoners and to keep them from maltreatment, but In India, we are yet envisioning for explicit acts to manage such issues. Indeed, even the jail manual drafted by boards and major recommendations contained in Justice Krishna Iyer Report on Women Prisoners, 1987, can't control the wrongdoings against women by caretakers. All in all, here the inquiry emerges who is to blame? Is it the lawmaking body, who have not sanctioned a particular enactment on violations done against women prisoners by custodians or is it the jail authorities, who are offered responsibility to restore those prisoners, however, they are absolutely conflicting with the morals of jail.

CRIMES AGAINST WOMEN

In spite of the fact that women might be victims of any of the general wrongdoings, for example, 'murder', 'theft', 'cheating', and so on, just the violations which are coordinated explicitly against women are portrayed as 'crimes against women'.

India is the most unsafe nation for sexual violence against women, as indicated by the Thomson Reuters Foundation 2018 survey.[8] The study, which estimates sexual and non-sexual violence, discrimination, social customs, medicinal services and human trafficking, has been condemned for reflecting more observation than information. In any case, India scarcely fares better in different examinations that rank its treatment of women. It is placed at 111st of 152 nations in the Georgetown Institute's global ranking of women's inclusion and well-being. India's National Crime Records Bureau revealed 118,954 crimes against women-including 18,947 rapes in 2016, the latest government information accessible. That is up from 109,546 reported incidents of violence against women in 2011.

One reason India has not had the capacity to successfully address crimes against women is the absence of women in national political office. That is on the grounds that, research shows, having women in government can prompt more and better laws that safeguards women's well-being. India's populace is 48 percent female. Be that as it may, women hold just under 12 percent of seats in the national legislature. That falls well underneath the 10 percent 'critical mass' that the United Nations Equal Opportunity Commission accepts is important for women law-makers to be powerful in policy-making.

Local governments in India really have an amount framework that guarantees women hold 11% of seats in rural and city councils. Be that as it may, female portrayal in India is unmistakably increasingly ground-breaking, national government stays practically identical to nations like the Republic of Congo and Mauritius, where women hold around 11 percent of legislative seats. Research exhibits that administrations that incorporate representatives from across society - that is, of various ideological groups, races, classes, sexual orientations, geologies and religions - produce better personal satisfaction for residents than less comprehensive governments. In New Zealand, where women hold 18 percent of parliamentary seats and the prime minister is a woman, lawmakers recently ensured paid leave for victims of domestic violence. That gives victims time to move, shielding themselves and their children from their abusers. Women in the United States Congress have additionally proactively tended to sexual harassment inside government. In March, female legislators from both the parties - who make up 22 percent of the U.S. Senate-drove Senate authority to call a vote on legislation that would give lawful portrayal to women who complain of sexual harassment on Capitol Hill and diminish boundaries to documenting a formal complaint. The bill passed in May, and is as of now being accommodated with the House's variant of a similar bill. Also, it was the late Chief Minister of India's Tamil Nadu state, J. Jayalalithaa, who in 2010 declared an 11-point activity plan for the state to better secure sexual violence survivors. Her arrangements, which have since been partially implemented, included state-paid medical expenses after abuse, female investigating officers and fast-track courts for sexual violence cases. India's 2011 national enactment on sexual savagery disregards a large number of these unfortunate victims' rights issues, as the human rights organizations Human Rights Watch and Amnesty International have pointed out.

Regarding rape and torture of woman, there are several cases where the apex court of India has put its' own observations. In *People's Union for Civil Liberties v Union of India &Another*, [9] it observes: 'undoubtedly, this court has been entertaining petition after petition involving the allegations of fake encounters and rapes by police personnel of states and in a large number of cases transferred the investigation itself to other agencies and particularly the CBI'. In *Francis Coralie Mullin v Administrator, U.T. of Delhi*, [10] it held: '.... any form of crimes and torture or cruel, inhuman or degrading treatment would be offensive to human dignity and constitute an inroad into this right to live and it would, on this view, be prohibited by Article 21 unless it is in accordance with procedure prescribed by law, but no law which authorizes and no procedure which leads to such crimes and torture or cruel, inhuman cr degrading treatment can ever stand the test of reasonableness and non-arbitrariness: it would plainly be unconstitutional and void as being violative of Articles 14 and 21.' In the case of *Mehboob Batcha v. State,* [11] ' the respondent policemen wrongfully confined one Nandagopal in police custody on suspicion of theft from 10.5.1992 till 2.6.1992 and beat him to death with lathis, and also gang raped his wife Padmini in a barbaric manner. The accused also confined several other persons (who were witnesses) and beat them in the police station with lathis. The graphic description of the barbaric conduct of the accused in this case shocked the conscience of the Court and it observed that policemen must learn how to behave as public servants in a democratic country, and not as oppressors of the people.' In Nandini Satpathy case,[12] it was observed that: 'not only physical threats or violence but psychological crimes and torture, atmospheric pressure, environmental coercion, tiring interrogation by police are violation of law.' In *Dagdu & Ors v State of Maharashtra*,[13] it was observed that 'if the custodians of law themselves indulge in committing crimes then no member of the society is safe and secure. If police officers who have to provide security and protection to the citizens indulge in such methods they are creating a sense of insecurity in the minds of the citizens. It is more heinous than a game-keeper becoming a poacher.' In the landmark case of Sheela Barse,[14] the Supreme Court laid down guidelines regarding arrest in general, and arrest of women in particular. The Court directed that 'four or five police lock-up should be reserved for female suspects and they should be kept away from the male suspects and be guarded by female constables; interrogation of females should be carried out only in the presence of female police officers/ constables; the District Judge would make surprise visits to police lock ups periodically with a view to providing the arrested persons an opportunity to air their grievances and ascertaining what are the conditions in the police lock ups and whether the requisite facilities are being provided and the provisions of law are being observed and the directions given by us are being carried out and the magistrate before whom an arrested person is produced shall enquire from the arrested person whether he has any complaint of Crimes and torture or mal-treatment in police custody and inform him that he has right under Section 54 of the CrPC, 1971 to be medically examined.'

From the above it is observed that woman has experienced different sorts of crimes and torture in Indian context. Apex judiciary has lots of concern due to emergence of several cases time to time. It provides necessary directives. The question is to what extent such directives and orders are followed in the ground level. It will become a vex issue when law enforcement agencies itself is involved in custodial crimes. A comprehensive road map and its' proper implementation is required to minimize crime and torture of different forms against women.

END NOTES

1. Editorial, "Rape every 20 minutes for the World's Largest Democracy" *Forbes,* Feb 01, 2011
2. Editorial, 'India's rape victim dies' *CBC News*, Apr 10, 2011
3. *Sunil Batra* vs. *Delhi Administration*, AIR 1978 SC 1575
4. 1981 AIR 178 by Justice PN Bhagwati
5. By Estelle R. Ramey
6. *TNN* Mar 8, 2011
7. Prison Conditions, *available at*: http://www.pucl.org/from-archives/81nov/jails.htm (Visited on February 15, 2020)
8. The World's Most Dangerous Countries for Women, *available at*: http://poll2018.trust.org. (Visited on February 16, 2020)
9. AIR 2005 SC 2419; (See also: *Dilip K. Basu* v. *State of W.B. & Ors*. AIR 1997 SC 1017 and *N.C. Dhoundial* v. *Union of India & Ors*. AIR 2004 SC 127; *Rubabbuddin Sheikh* v. *State of Gujarat & Ors*. AIR 2010 SC 1175; *Jaywant P. Sankpal* v. *Suman Gholap & Ors.,* (2010) 11 SCC 208; and *Narmada Bai* v. *State of Gujarat & Ors*., (2011) 5 SCC 79)
10. AIR 1981 SC 746
11. (2011) 7 SCC 45
12. *Nandini Satpathy* v. *P.L Dani &Anr.*, AIR 1978 SC 1025
13. AIR 1977SC1579
14. *Sheela Barse* v *State of Maharashtra*, AIR 1981 SC 178

6

An Evaluative Study of Sexual Harassment of Women at Work-place (Prevention, Prohibition and Redressal) Act, 2013

Yash Singh Sisodiya

In India, sexual harassment at work environment is one of the most widely recognized violations against female and is likewise observed as illegal encroaching of the fundamental right of women. In some cases women take a stand against such shameful act however in the majority of cases it is buried with time. For preventing such injustice and to systematic deal with such cases, the Sexual Harassment Act, 2013 was enacted. The Act clarifies as to what constitutes sexual harassment, what is a workplace and who shall be considered aggrieved along with some guidelines on how work environments should be proactive about guaranteeing that the security of women. This is an attempt to clarify the thin line between the act's provision and contradictory loopholes through critical evaluation of the act.

INTRODUCTION

The Act, 2013 enacted 16 years after the decision of Supreme court of India (*Vishaka & Ors v State of Rajasthan & Ors*, 1997) which define it as sexually moved behaviour which is not welcomed by other gender includes-physical advances (unwelcomed), sexual favours, coloured remarks, showing pornography, any verbal and non-verbal gestures or conduct of sexual in nature. The objective is to prevent, protect and provide redressal mechanism to women at the workplace. Recently there has been a complaint by lady for sexual harassment in court premises by the judge by former employee accusing him of making unwanted sexual advances (Krishnan, 2019) and in another case, a senior Air India pilot was accused by a woman colleague for sexual harassment was found guilty by an internal committee (Times, 2020). Sexual harassment at workplace may result in undermines victim's self-respect and thus result in psychological trauma that leads to the unfavorable hostile working environment (Shaw, 2018) and can cause harm individual both physically as well as psychologically (Singh, 2016).

Regardless of consideration in the news and mainstream society, sexual harassment is not well understood. 45 percent of men and 70 percent of women report being subjected to relevant offensive behaviors in the workplace (Amy 2012) so it is very important to address the most ignored aspect of act and explore practical ways to minimize the non-reporting and make act more effective on ground.

BACKGROUND

It all starts with the case of Banwari Devi, a women activist stop child marriage in Rajasthan and faces rape on the field in form of retaliation by upper-class men. The group of women activist named Vishaka filed PIL to inform the Supreme Court to take into account women safety at workplace resulted in what is popularly known as the Vishakha Guidelines.

The judgment of August 1997 provided the basic definitions of sexual harassment at the workplace with guidelines to deal with it which includes employer's responsibility, complaint mechanism, complaint committee, etc. It was considered as the first legal victory specifically to addresses sexual harassment at the workplace and thus harassment came to be considered as offence (Rodrigues 2014). Supreme Court gave 12 pointer guidelines known as Vishaka guidelines (Sengar 2014). Sexual harassment bill introduced in 2007 got approved in 2010 and then with some amendments in 2012 and finally enacted on December 9, 2013. Banwari Devi case reached globally and hence Vishaka judgement was accorded with CEDAW (Convention on the Elimination of all form of Discrimination against Women) (Pandey, 2016).

LITERATURE REVIEW

There are various reports on sexual harassment on the basis of the study at the workplace across the world. In his exploratory study at Lebanon (Hejase 2015) attempts to close the gap of very less recorded cases in public domain and cases that take place. Here comparative analysis can be done on Indian culture because in Lebanon also any word, expression in a speech from opposite sex said aggressively not considered sexual harassment yet. He further explains that sexual harassment at the workplace affects man and woman differently. Dang (2017) performs his study on a woman on a high post in the organisation. And provide three important pillars of organisational harassment prevention i.e. (gender sensitivity, zero tolerance and socialisation). Bhat (2017) identifies the most frequent acts done by perpetrators to maintain their power position. He explains the causes of sexual harassment at the workplace with the help of data. Dhanasekar (2018) focused their study on women of information technology and business process outsourcing (BPO) and shows that 88% ladies in BPO and IT feels some kind of humiliating working environment at workplace particularly in private institutions. Consider the Act itself a loophole. Unnikrishnan *et al.* (2010) in their cross-sectional study of Karnataka demonstrate that most vulnerable section who faces harassment are young girls especially girls in the sales profession. Based on some literature review regarding sexual harassment of women at workplace issue we can assume a rise in cases shown by the National Crime Records Bureau. There is a rise of almost 30% cases between 2017 and 2018 (Chauhan 2020) shows that women maintain their faith in justice system.

THEORETICAL FRAMEWORK

Sexual harassment at the workplace can be defined as the humiliating act or behaviour which is considered inappropriate at the workplace situation. Between 2014 and 2017, there is a 54% rise in cases of sexual harassment at the workplace (Alphonso 2018). If some surveys compiled it can be said that four out of five women did not report harassment to their employer (Khan 2018) and particularly in Indian context a woman is harassed sexually every 12 minutes (Singh 2016). The data is already alarming and still, there are majority of cases that are non reported and data suggest that about 78% of cases go unreported (Local Circles 2018). Women constitute 26.7% of the total workforce (PTI 2019) and constitute 48 per cent of the Indian population but not profited equally (World 2019) considered as strong pillar of Indian overall development and still faces more harassment comparatively most impacted are girls aged (14-20 years) followed by widow and divorced and lastly the girls with low educational background (Sengar 2014). Similarly when it comes to academics or teaching workplace, data suggests that incidents of sexual harassment are common in medical, engineering and academic sciences and medical students face it more frequently (National Academics of Sciences 2018).

RATIONALE, OBJECTIVE AND METHODOLOGY

Even after the enactment of the Act, there are very low awareness and even lower reporting rate. Recently cases of sexual harassment in different NGOs and freelancing employees that came into public notice which shows that although the introductions of sexual harassment act on the ground there is more alarming conditions that require the overall evaluation of the act along with the study of other qualitative dimensions. The present endeavour is a descriptive study to know about impact and shortcomings in the act and identify the attempts made for the identification of incidents of sexual harassment at the workplace at different situations and analyse the act with a focus on the causes that lead perpetrators to harass and victim to be harassed by using secondary sources of information like journals, informative video blogs, government reports and news articles related to sexual harassment of women at workplace and analyse the act through literature review and reliable data with the purpose to evaluate the Act and provide practical suggestions. The study is categorized into three divisions: identification of reasons for non-reporting of cases, identify some ignored loopholes in the act and make practical measures/suggestions to solve the problems faced by different stakeholders.

DISCUSSION ON THE ACT

The Act defines 'sexual harassment' as unwelcome acts such as physical contact, demand for sexual favours, showing pornography, sexually coloured remarks and any other acts including verbal, non-verbal that is sexual in nature. The act is applicable to all India and includes both organised and unorganised sector (Poonia 2019). The unorganised workplace includes less than 10 workers and places where service rules are not applicable (Desai 2019). As a matter of fact, the condition of the unorganised sector is even worse where employees with a lack of rules and guidelines compelled to work (Hejase 2015). In rural India there are still division of stratification and unorganized labour is highly stratified on basis of community and caste and the awareness regarding redressal is very less and that sometimes make women susceptible to incidents of sexual harassment at unorganised sectors (Talkitover). Subsequently the act mandates companies to constitute internal complaint committee (section 4) and local committee (section 6) for domestic harassment (dwelling place or house) and unorganised workplaces. However when it comes to redressal at ground level, local committee has wider scope than internal complaint committee (Sarpotdar 2020). Furthermore act also provides the extended workplace provision which includes transportation and places visited to fulfil employment role. Act also widen the definition of employee and aggrieved women which include any women employed or not, of any age and subject to harassment at workplace and even the visitor or customer are also included in POSH act (Poonja 2018). Subsequently, act mandates employer to assure a safe working environment under their jurisdiction and if any case comes to him he should help the victim with proper redressal either through conciliation or investigation (Desai 2019).

REASON FOR NON-REPORTING

Fear of not taken seriously is a big reason (Singh 2016) that is why respondent chooses not to approach the authority because in India there is prejudice attached with the female of faulty reporting and some insensitive nature of questions stop victim further to resist the harassment and thus repetition creates life pattern and perpetrator saw this as a normal incident (Rodrigues, 2014). Women lack confidence in our justice system due to inappropriate uncomfortable interview questions and long pendency of the cases (Dhanasekar 2018) bill itself takes 20 years to become an act so it'll be very difficult to expect anything like timely justice from authorities in charge. Taboo attached to Indian culture for non-reporting and that expect women to adjust with consequences and thus perpetrators go free that further leads to professional victimisation and economical abuse that is with low awareness of job role and frequent requirement of superior support make sexual harassment normal in return of job security (Khan 2018). There's a very famous quote that says justice delayed is justice denied that sometimes become an obstacle in form of non-reporting of cases. Therefore such incidents can cause deep harm and not only it affects victim physically but more mentally and can put her in grave risk of depression or post-traumatic stress disorder (Shaw et al 2018).

POSITIVE ASPECTS

The act provides prevention, prohibition of sexual acts and redressal mechanism for women at workplace. This was great victory of women issues activism. There was great provision in the act that explains that after disposal of the case for 5 years close watch should be kept on victim to ensure her safety. 2018 (KelpHR 2018) survey indicates that 77% organisations are fully compliant with the act in India. Out of them 45% finds their workplace safer and 91% shows increased awareness and therefore this act is said to be positive addition to Vishaka guidelines.

LOOPHOLES

Section 14(1) of act that prescribes punishment for false complaint and evidence also keep actual victim away from reporting due to lack of evidence therefore potential complainant remain left out (Sarpotdar 2020). Inadequate evidence doesn't mean false complain there is thin line of act that can be trap to victim himself. It is one of the reasons of non reporting that victim not able to produce direct evidence (ibid). Time limit of reporting limit of cases is 3 months provided by section 9(1) after that Delhi Local committee dismiss the case. Jurisdiction issue still persist in the act that raises confusion on part of complainant. Recently Karnataka Local committee rejects complaint because incident not falls under their jurisdiction (ibid). Most common issue regarding the act is gender specificity focus explicitly and exclusively on female victims (Prashanti 2020). In the study by Hejase (2015), it is found that out of all cases of sexual harassment at workplace male faces 12% and female 16% of incidents with only 5% reporting from both the genders. And furthermore there are under representation of male sexual harassment studies. Dang (2017) provide useful analysis of the problem in reporting process and put forward that sometimes complaint mechanism is more problematic than incident itself.

IMPACT AND IMPLICATIONS

There is a large number of studies available that shows that sexual harassment issue is faced by every gender but studies show majority of them are female and it effect on genders are also different (Kim 2018). In most cases action taken by female is to quit job whereas men just got their transfer to another department (Hejase 2015). Likewise, for female gender the effects are different because they find difficult to adjust and tend to feel their work atmosphere as a hostile, unhealthy and thus produce less productive outcome (Dhanasekar 2018). Sengar (2014) provide the list of most impacted section in which female girls aged (14-20 years) followed by widow and divorced and lastly the girls with low educational background are more vulnerable. Among them divorced and separated women more likely to experience the incidents of harassment at workplace and females work in lower organisational hierarchy experience almost the same level of harassment at workplace. According to Sakshi survey (2001) and Yugantar Educational Society (2003) sexual harassment cases can cause a loss in work productivity, depression and mistrust (Dang 2017).

MEASURES AND SUGGESTIONS

Sexual harassment issue needs to be a part of political campaign along with cultural awakening of society in general and children in particular (Shaw J). Internal complaint committee should include employees of every class in hierarchy so it becomes easily accessible to victim. Self employed and freelancer workers should also be given due recognition with clear description on their side. Although there are clauses mentioned in the act but not clear (Madell 2018). Some provisions of the act need more interpretations like perpetrators criteria, conciliation, and victim with less or no evidence etc. Investigation committee can include psychologist (mind reader) and social researcher (observer) on the members list so that it'll be convenient to find various hidden meanings in interviews. Prevention should be focused because preparation and implementation of preventive measures take less time than investigation process. There should be compulsory action and applied research based policy at every office and organisation to address local issues. Educational institutions and offices should from the start practise gender diverse work environment to increase productivity (ibid Dang). Ensure women representation at every level with great gender and racial equality in hiring and promotions (National Academies of Sciences, National Academic Press, 2018). Although India currently has only 11% women in parliament whereas our neighbour Pakistan has 20% rate even Rwanda has highest (63.8%) participation (Rodrigues 2014).

CONCLUSION

The study is based on secondary research method and this approach would not necessarily fill some of the research gaps, but helps to provide broad understanding of the POSH act and its critical evaluation at initial level. In present times India has seen more women participation in workforce like never before so it become important to raise awareness of sexual harassment at workplace. Enactment of long pending act of 2013 is great way forward to protect women from harassment and provide systematic redressal. In today's modern society women have started taking up influential positions which might seen as challenge to the men who is socialised around patriarchal societal structure therefore attempt to rule them through harassment. However, Vishaka cases provide strict guidelines only after that the Supreme Court view it as violation of fundamental right of equality in general and gender equality in particular. Advantages of acts need to balance themselves with its disadvantages. Further research on this area makes it more effective on grass root implementation.

REFERENCES

Alphonso, M. a. (2018, October 15). *Indiaspend.com*. Retrieved July 14, 2020, from *India Spend* : https://www.indiaspend.com/metooindia-54-rise-in-sexual-harassment-reported-at-workplaces-between-2014-17/

Amy, B. (2012, MAY). Fighting Sexual Harassment in the workplace. *Scholars Strategy Network*, p. 1.

Bhat, A. (2017). An Overview of Sexual Harassment of Women. *International Journal of Innovative Research in Science,*, 10.

Chauhan, N. (2020, january 9). *www.hindustantimes.com*. Retrieved july 14, 2020, from Hindustan times : https://www.hindustantimes.com/india-news/30-rise-in-sexual-abuse-of-young-women-in-shelter-homes-ncrb-annual-report/story-OApm3FPeP0ZUsha5IWdKuK.html#:~:text=According%20to%20the%20latest%20government,instances%20reported%20the%20previous%20year.

Dang, S. A. (2017). Sexual Harassment of Women at workplace expreience of women managers and organizations. *Economic and Political Weekly*

Desai. (2019). India's law on prevention of sexual harassment at the workplace. *Nishith Desai assosiateslegal and tax counselling*, 4.

Dhanasekar, R. A. (2018). A Study on sexal harassment of women at workplace in India. *International journal of pure and applied mathematics*.

Hejase, H. J. (2015). Sexual Harassment in Workplace : An Exploratory study from Lebanon. *Journal of Management Research*.

Kelp, HR. (2018, september 17). *kelphr.com*. Retrieved july 12, 2020, from https://www.kelphr.com/: https://www.kelphr.com/blogs/advantages-and-disadvantages-of-posh-act/

Khan, T. (2018). Sexual Harassment of Women at Workplace. *International Journal of Law Management & Humanities*, 15-16.

Kim, P. (2018, March 7). *Gender discrimination more common for women*. Retrieved july 15, 2020, from pewresearch.org: https://www.pewresearch.org/fact-tank/2018/03/07/women-in-majority-male-workplaces-report-higher-rates-of-gender-discrimination/

Krishnan, M. (2019, April 25). *dw.com*. Retrieved july 14, 2020, from DW made for minds: https://www.dw.com/en/india-supreme-court-rattled-by-sexual-harassment-case/a-48463877.

LocalCircles. (2018, October 16). *LocalCircles.com*. Retrieved JULY 14, 2020, from LocalCircles: https://www.localcircles.com/a/press/page/metoo-sexual-harassment-in-india#.Xw3uEDozYdV.

Madell, R. (2018, April 2). *flexjobs.com*. Retrieved july 12, 2020, from flexjobs: https://www.flexjobs.com/blog/post/freelancers-self-employed-not-immune-harassment/

National Academies of Sciences, E. a. (2018). National Academic Press. Retrieved July 7, 2020, from National Academic Press: https://www.nap.edu/nap-cgi/skimchap.cgi?recid=24994&chap=189-210.

National Academies of Sciences, E. a. (2018). *Sexual Harassment of women Climate, Culture, and Consequences in Academic Sciences, Engineering, and Medicine.* Washington, DC: The National Academies Press.

Pandey, A. K. (2016, September 17). *India Times.* Retrieved JULY 14, 2020, from www.indiatimes.com: https://www.indiatimes.com/news/all-you-need-to-know-about-the-bhanwari-devi-case-that-led-to-the-formation-of-the-vishakha-guidelines-261665.html

Poonia. (2019). Sexual Harassment at Workplace. *Amity International Journal of Juridical Sciences.*

Poonja, M. a. (2018, june 27). *india-posh-act-a-snapshot.* Retrieved july 15, 2020, from accdocket.com: https://www.accdocket.com/articles/india-posh-act-a-snapshot.cfm#:~:text=The%20Act%20recognizes%20that%20sexual,environment%20free%20from%20sexual%20harassment.

Prashanti. (2012). *Legal service india.* Retrieved july 12, 2020, from Legal service india : http://www.legalservicesindia.com/article/2039/Sexual-Harassment-of-Men.html

PTI. (2019, MARCH 8). *thehindu.com.* Retrieved JULY 14, 2020, from The Hindu : https://www.thehindu.com/business/female-labour-force-participation-in-india-fell-to-26-in-2018-report/article26467857.ece#

Rodrigues, P. &. (2014). Sexual Harassment at Workplace in India Medico-Legal Aspects. Journal of Indian Academy of Foreignsic Medicine, 3

Sarpotdar, A. (2020). Examining Local Committees under the Sexual Harassment of Women at Workplace Act. *Economic and Political weekly.*

Sengar (2014). Analysis on Sexual Harassment of Women. *International Journal of Law and Legal Jurisprudence Studies*, 7

Shaw et al., 2. (2018). Sexual Harassment and Assault at Work: Understanding the Costs. *The Institute for Women's Policy Research.*

Shaw, H. H. (2018). Sexual Harassment and Assault at Work: Understanding the Costs. *The Institute for Women's Policy Research*, 5.

Shaw, J. The untold story of witnesses of workplace harassment. *TEDx talks.* TEDxLondonWomen, London.

Singh. (2016). Prevention of Sexual Harassment of Women in the. *The Journal of International Women's Studies*, 104-105.

Talkitover. (n.d.). *talkitover.in.* Retrieved JULY 15, 2020, from Talk It Over Counselling: https://talkitover.in/consultation/preventing-sexual-harassment/how-secure-are-women-working-in-the-unorganized-sectors

Times, E. (2020, January 19). *economictimes.indiatimes.com.* Retrieved July 14, 2020, from Economic Times, : https://economictimes.indiatimes.com/topic/Genpact-sexual-harassment-case

Unnikrishnan *et al.,* 2. (2010). Harassment among Women at Workplace: A Cross-Sectional Study in Coastal South India. *The Indian Journal of Community Medicine.*

Wikipedia, T. F. (2020, June 26). *Tarana Burke*. Retrieved 7 7, 2020, from wikipedia: https://en.wikipedia.org/wiki/Tarana_Burke

World, B. (2019, March 8). *worldbank.org*. Retrieved JULY 14, 2020, from World Bank: https://www.worldbank.org/en/news/feature/2019/03/08/working-for-women-in-india.

7

Crime and Atrocities on Women: The Saga of Partition

Anshumi Chowdhury

Among many events of history which kept people engrossed and is equally intriguing is the history of partition. For ages, many works have been produced in this line. In fact, knowledge of the basic ideas or events related to partition is known to most of the laymen. However, for a long time, only the political developments surrounding partition was given much importance. And the underlying events which caused great distress to the people who suffered partition, for a long time was avoided. One such is the plight of women during and after partition that came to the forefront some 40-50 years later. Like many others, they not only had to face the problem of displacement, migration, rehabilitation, among many others but also had to face extreme violence, torture, public humiliation, rape, murder and abduction. However, it was the numerous cases of abduction of women which ultimately got some political light and accordingly a Bill and finally an Act was passed by the Parliament of India. These violated women on both sides had to face some serious trouble of every form which needs proper discussion to throw light on social behaviour and to understand partition from their perspective.

INTRODUCTION

The year 1947 saw both victory and loss. Victory in the form of independence of India from the British Raj and loss in the form of deaths, displacement and violence because of the partition that followed. For a very long time, the central emphasis of partition was documenting and glorifying the Independence and also writing about the displacement and loss of people. It was much later that the plight of women during and since partition was given due importance. This is because women were mostly portrayed in these historical writings as objects of study rather than subjects [1]. Many untold miseries of women now gained the amount of light it required and as a result the hardships, sufferings and anguish of women tormented during partition were being catalogued. History gaining momentum by analyzing the marginalized section of the society under subaltern studies and also the rise of feminist historiography gave the exact amount of push to understand and write about the problems faced specifically by women during the partition of India. Mostly being described as the vulnerable section of the society, they faced not only the problems related to displacement but also had to take the brunt of the confusion and frustrations on their shoulders in the form of various kind of violence which include, rape, abduction, torture, murder etc. One of the most important questions that arise here is that, India's struggle for freedom saw many women participation in public sphere and in politics, so how can these women are subjugated by males or are violated. There were indeed many cases of women participation in various movements prior to India's independence during colonial supremacy. But to remind us, majority of them came from humble background and at the end of the day when they go home they had to play the role of a wife, mother, sister etc, and were termed as domestic beings. And even though they got themselves involved in political scenarios but ultimately they were bind-up in this patriarchal set up where they were considered as inferior to their male counterparts. Although the colonial India saw women participation in public sphere but such large-scale violation and torture on women during partition was a direct result of the stereotypical notion that they are only the biological reproducers for the community and symbol of communal boundaries[2].

However, with time many literary works were produced highlighting partition as viewed by women and the silent trauma they faced, such as; *Jhootha Sach* by Yashpal, *Ice-Candy Man* by Bapsi Sidhwa, *Azadi* by Chaman Nahal, *Epar Ganga, Opar Ganga* (The River Churning) by Jyotirmoyee Devi, *The Other side of Silence: Voices from the Partition of India* by Urvashi Butalia, *Borders and Boundaries: Women in India's Partition* by Ritu Menon and Kamla Bhasin etc. Adding to this, oral narratives and interviews of partition survivors were the essential sources used with time by many scholars and curious enthusiasts to understand the partition from the perspective of women. Although, India was divided into east (present Bangladesh) and west Pakistan and the atrocities on both the sides are equally important but this paper will discuss the plight of women mostly concerning western border and the areas nearby. This was done so as to reduce the vastness of the work and to concentrate on a single area in utmost details.

OBJECTIVES AND METHODOLOGY

Key objectives of this endeavor is to highlight the different forms of atrocities on women during partition, to trace the motives behind such violence against women and to throw light on the plight of abducted women in partition. The present work is based on a socio-historical approach and is qualitative in nature. Also, an intensive and extensive study has been attempted in order to cover the topic. The work is completely based on secondary sources which include books, journals, articles, research papers etc. subjecting them to both internal and external criticism.

OVERVIEW AND FINDINGS

Partition was an event which was unfortunate on the part of many people. As for women, atrocities upon them started even before the dreadful event. Considering this and the communal violence that was happening and was going to happen in huge number after partition, the Indian National Congress passed a resolution in their 1946 session at Meerut by Dr. Rajendra Prasad and seconded by Maulana Abdul Kalam Azad [3]. However, the cases of abducted women and the terrible violence that they faced came to the forefront after partition when family members began to lodge complains about their missing women from household. And the government also decided to take some action against it. An estimated figure of 80,000 to 150,000 women were said to be abducted during this time[4].The brutality that the womenfolk faced came from two sources, one was the violence done by men of other communal groups and the other was the violence inflicted by their own community or family. Kamlaben Patel, a social-worker who worked closely with raped and abducted women at partition recalled the various kinds of violence inflicted on them:

Apart from rape, other specific kind of violence had been visited on women. Many were paraded naked on the streets, several had their breasts cut-off, their bodies were tattooed with marks of 'other' religion, in a bid to defile the so-called 'purity' of the race, women were forced to have sex with men of other religion, and many were impregnated .[5] This was the gruesome scenario of violence inflicted on women by other communal groups. The purity of a woman is connected to the purity of the whole family, community and sometimes nation. Therefore, this kind of violence occurred mostly as an indirect blow to the men folk of the rival communal group and also to the nation that they supported. As a result a woman's body became the perfect model where one group tried to prove their religious dominance over the other [6]. Also, this type of brutality is a touchstone of how the sexuality of women played an important part in understanding gender relations in this patriarchal set-up and within religious communities [7]. On asking Kamlaben why she choose to keep quite or did not write about her experience for decades, she answered it by saying that she saw partition as a 'tandav nritya' [8]. Even many families who faced such horrible atrocities directly or indirectly did not wish to talk about it. Such an attitude might be an indication towards them being ashamed of such things. Women are considered to hold the dignity of a family and anything bad happening to them might mean burnt on the dignity of the whole family, or even the whole community.

So far violence against women of other community is being discussed. However, there were also innumerable cases where violence against one's own womenfolk by their men and even women themselves dominated the scene. Safeguarding the honour of one's religion and community was the prime concern during partition and in some cases till date. It has been known that a number of women and children were strangled, poisoned, burnt to death, drowned or put to sword, also women used to burnt, strangulate and shot themselves and their daughter, which also went to the extreme of eating opium or crushed glasses to attain death [9]. This type of violence was performed mostly as to save the honour, purity and sanctity of one's family or community as a woman is always portrayed associated with such expressions. In the same line, another famous mass suicide was committed by 90 women of the village of Thoa Khalsa of Rawalpindi district by drowning themselves in a well to save their honour by being raped or forced conversion [10]. This news was first published in the English newspaper by the name *The Statesman*. Thus, suicide was another alternative applied willingly by the womenfolk to save themselves. The women of Thoa Khalsa who committed suicides are till date applauded and they were given respect considering the sacrifice that they did. Honorable deaths by women in the form of *sati* or *jauhar* were applauded. And such practices were another motivation for the women of partition to go in that line too. Although they did it by themselves but it is questionable that, were such deaths also to be accounted as a form of violence, because women since long were ear-fed, brainwashed to do such act and were made the only figure metaphorically representing the honour of her family, community, religion etc.

Added to this was the plight of abducted women. Taking into consideration the huge complaints about missing women who were abducted, the All India Congress Committee passed a resolution on 17th November 1947 to bring back abducted women and on December 6th 1947, both the Indian and Pakistani government signed an Inter-Dominion Treaty to recover such abducted women on both sides [11]. Although the steps were taken to recover these abducted women, but the major question that arose out of this was how to determine who were abducted and who were not. According to the government, the violence in Punjab began as early as March of 1947 and therefore it was anonymously decided that those women who were seen or are witnessed living with a man of other religion after March 1 of 1947 were to be believed as abducted [12]. The partition gave every citizen the right to choose the nation where they prefer to stay but as for the case of abducted women had no say in this. They were ordered by the government to be returned to the nation of their respective religion or community. Also, the Ordinance of Abducted person's Recovery and Restoration was at first transformed into a Bill and later in 1949 was made into an Act. During the same time a book was published by the A. J .Fletcher containing the list of abducted women and children from India both young and old and according to it most of the abductors were from the same village or community, and as for the abduction of older women were done mostly to acquire their property by making these women their mother or any other relation [13]. Added to this was the psychological violence that these women had to go through. The government of India passed an ordinance, according to which: "Those (Hindu) women whose babies were born in Pakistan after partition would have to leave them behind, but those (Muslim) whose children were born in India, could keep them."[14]

While the government of both the countries were trying to bring back abducted women to their respective nation, another problem related to this arose in India. As for Pakistan, the women who survived a family were willingly accepted back. But this was not in the case of India. As mentioned above, the concept of purity and honour of a woman was given much importance in the Hindu and Sikh community. Therefore, those abducted women were now considered as impure or polluted having gone through conversion and rape and a child born out of such mixed union was always considered by the society as impure[15]. Even Nehru and Gandhi both spoke publicly trying to erase the concept of impurity from the minds of people and urged these families to accept back their women. However, even after many attempts such women still were not taken back by their families and they were rehabilitated by the government and given shelter in Ashrams. In the course of time many ashrams opened up to accommodate such women.

Another problem that the government faced was the unwillingness of a few women to return back to their respective nation. The very first reason for doing so was that after settling in the new environment since abduction, these women were now comfortable with their surroundings. These women brought themselves to come in term with their new surrounding and saw the recovery programme as an act of their second abduction[16]. Taking into consideration the case of a lady, who was sold by her father to a police officer from Pakistan in exchange of being able to reach safely to the cantonment in India [17]. This was another reason that such abducted women did not want to return back to their families who thought their womenfolk as commodities to be sold and exchanged. This brought light to cases of many police officers who themselves abducted many women and because of which the operation of recovery ran slow and without much lead for many years. Also, sometimes a woman sees her abductor as her saviour. By 1957, estimates of 30,000 women were recovered[18]. This is because in such a situation of turmoil, with all her family killed or disappeared, she views her abductor as an angel who although abducted her but also gave her food and shelter[19]. However, many feminist scholars have criticized the initiative on the part of the government to being back these abducted women. According to them, a women found in the household of other community was taken as an abducted women after March 1, 1947, without taking into consideration her wish or her willingness. Secondly, they believed that many coercive tactics were applied to bring back such women[20]. Also, many oral narratives of the social workers involved in such restoration programme claimed that when they find such women unwilling to go home, they tried hard to convince them to return and eventually in many cases they did succeeded in doing so. One such was the famous love story from partition, which found place in both Urvashi Butalia's work, *The other side of silence* and in *Partition dialogues*, as narrated by Krishna Sobti to Alok Bhalla. The love story was between Buta Singh, a Sikh and Zainab, a Muslim. As mentioned by Butalia through research, Zainab was abducted from a caravan headed to Pakistan. From there she was sold to many men and finally to Buta Singh. However, Buta Singh and Zainab fell in love and they married each other. But their happiness was short-lived as both the nations entered into Inter-Dominion Treaty and the programme of recovery of abducted women had started. With this Zainab was also taken back to Pakistan without her wish.

Many debates were made in honour of the plight of tortured, raped, brutalized and abducted women. But very few works discussed the trauma of perpetrators. Deepti Misri discusses about the short story from *Sharifan* of Saadat Hasan Manto, where she critically analyses the character of Qasim who gets prompted after seeing the naked and violated dead body of his daughter Sarifan after getting home, so in a fit of rage he goes out to kill the Sikhs and the Hindu men and also sexually violated the daughter of the Hindu neighbour in the same manner as his daughter had experienced [21]. However, this kind of doings does not allow or open any scope to sympathize the perpetrator for their heinous crimes but at the same time also highlights the trauma faced by them. Also, the fate of Sarifan is symbolic of the plight of women who were uselessly dragged to the surface of tension.

Even though much initiative was taken on the part of India to bring back abducted women but not much attention was given to their rehabilitation programme. As already discussed much of these women were rejected by their family and thus government could do nothing but to open ashrams to accommodate them. They were also provided with opportunities to work in factories and industrial units, but the income they received was meagre. Their future prospect of getting married was also in oblivion.

The next big question that arises out of all these debates was, why was the recovery of abducted women became a big question for India? Also, why were organizations like RSS and Akhil Bharatiya Hindu Mahasabha so interested in them? The answer to the first question lies in the core of India's condition at that time. India recently lost a part in the formation of East and West Pakistan. Therefore, the nation wanted to portray itself as a responsible state, the one that fulfils the concerns and duties towards its citizens and thus the recovery of abducted women became a big question for the Indian government. As for RSS and Akhil Bharatiya Hindu Mahasabha, the question of Hindu conversion into Christianity and Islam was of big concern and thus, they gave full interest in recovering these non-Muslim women from Pakistan. These women were seen as the target of conversion by such organizations and thus, were treated as a medium to propagate their philosophy[22]. Dey is of the opinion that as the post-colonial construct of Mother India became prominent, any attack on its women is considered as an attack on the nation, nation symbolizing as mother/women[23].

In the conclusion, it can be said that where a section of people were suffering from the after-effects and problems of partition like dislocation, violence, rehabilitation, starvation, death etc, but at the same time along with these problems a section of women were suffering from additional violation which were gruesome in nature. Also, not only this but the abducted women had to suffer dual dislocation and humiliations and their children born out of mixed union were always treated as impure or polluted by the society. Most of these children were to be given out for adoption as for these abducted women had no other choice. However, for such recovered women the government now tried to make them economically independent by providing those jobs in industries for spinning, weaving, etc. But one of the most important outcomes of partition is women empowerment with the emergence of refugee women and women either rejected by their families or having no family as makers of their own destiny. These women now became the sole-earner for themselves and did all sorts of jobs that they came across. In a way they became independent of male dominion which they might have faced living with their families. Sadly, the terrible atrocities on women prove that they were never considered of any importance by this patriarchal set-up other than being the flag-bearers of purity and honour and symbol of communal and national pride. And thus, their sexuality was treated either as vulnerable beings to be violated or as inferior beings to remain under the control of the society.

END NOTES

1. Menon, Ritu and Bhasin, Kamla. *Borders and Boundaries, Women in India's Partition*, p.11
2. Bhattacharyya, Arnab. *The Enigma of Partition towards a Literary Understanding*. p. 135
3. Menon, Ritu and Bhasin, Kamla. *op.cit.*, p. 68,69
4. Forbes, Geraldine. *Women in Modern India*. p. 224
5. Butalia, Urvashi. *The Other Side of Silence, Voices from the Partition of India*. p. 132
6. Dey, Arunima. *Violence against Women during the Partition of India: Interpreting Women and their Bodies in the Context of Ethnic Genocide*. p. 107
7. Menon, Ritu and Bhasin, Kamla, *op.cit.*, p. 41

8. Butalia, Urvashi, *op.cit.,* p. 133
9. Misri, Deepti. *Beyond Partition, Gender, Violence and representation in Postcolonial India.* p. 55,56
10. Pandey, Gyanendra. *Community and Violence: Recalling Partition.* p. 2041
11. Menon, Ritu and Bhasin, Kamla, *op.cit.,* p. 69
12. Butalia, Urvashi, *op.cit.,* p. 144
13. *ibid.,* p. 135, 136
14. Menon, Ritu and Bhasin, Kamla, *op.cit.,* p. 100, 101
15. Butalia, Urvashi, *op.cit.,* p. 160, 161
16. Forbes, Geraldine. *op.cit.,* p. 224
17. Menon, Ritu and Bhasin, Kamla, *op.cit.,* p. 78
18. Forbes, Geraldine. *op.cit.,* p. 224
19. Dey, Arunima. *op.cit.,* p. 111, 112
20. Bhattacharyya, Arnab. *op.cit.,* p. 141
21. Misri, Deepti. *op.cit.,* p. 34
22. Menon, Ritu and Bhasin, Kamla, *op.cit.,* p. 122, 123
23. Dey, Arunima. *op.cit.,* pp. 107-110

BIBLIOGRAPHY

Altekar, A.S. *The Position of Women in Hindu Civilization*. Motilal Banarsidass Publishers Pvt. Ltd: Delhi, 2016

Bandyopadhyay, Sekhar. *From Plassey to Partition and After.* Orient Blackswan Pvt Ltd, New Delhi, 2016

Bandyopadhyay, Sekhar. *Nationalist Movement in India*. Oxford University Press, New Delhi, 2009

Bhattacharyya, Arnab. *The Enigma of Partition towards a Literary Understanding*. Shoudhganga, http://hdl.handle.net/10603/197612, Chapter 3: Jadavpur University, accessed on 2 July 2020

Butalia, Urvashi. *The Other Side of Silence, Voices from the Partition of India.* Penguin Books India Pvt. Ltd, New Delhi, 1998. (web)

Chandra, Bipan. *India's Struggle for Independence*. Penguin Books, Haryana, 1989

Chandra, Bipan. *India since' Independence*. Penguin Books: Haryana, 2008 (printed)

Dey, Arunima. 'Violence against Women during the Partition of India: Interpreting Women and their Bodies in the Context of Ethnic Genocide'.

E.S. Revista de Filologia Inglesa, *Dialnet Journal*, 2016, accessed on 1 July 2020 (web).

Forbes, Geraldine. *Women in Modern India*. Cambridge University press, Delhi, 2015

Menon, Ritu and Bhasin, Kamla, *Borders and Boundaries, Women in India's Partition*. Kali for Women: Delhi, 1998 (web)

Misri, Deepti. *Beyond Partition, Gender, Violence and representation in Postcolonial India*. University of Illinois Press, Chicago, 2014 (web).

Pandey, Gyanendra. *Community and Violence: Recalling Partition. Economic and Political Weekly*, vol. 32, no.32, 1997, JSTOR, www.jstor.org/stable/ 4405734. Accessed on 1 July, 2020 (web)

8

Do Women Get Justice?

Pallavi Goswami

"We need women at all levels, including the top to change the dynamics, reshape the conversation to make sure women's voices are heard and heeded, not overlooked and ignored"

- Sheryl Sandberg

Crime against women is a major issue from time immemorial. Violence against women has taken the form of global epidemic, which has taken its toll on the physical, mental, sexual and economic life of the females. There are a lot of factors responsible for crime against women. The first and foremost factor is 'the mentality of our society. Our society still considers men as the superior and women as inferior. As it is said that charity begins at home, hence to reduce the crime rates against women we need to start it from our home. We need to change our mentality at first. At the out set, it is very important to clear out the basics about crime and the first thing that comes to our mind: what is crime? So the answer is: crime is a universal phenomenon. It is serious issue that is committed all over the world-somewhere less & somewhere more. It is an act that is harmful for the society. Nelson Mandela said 'when a man is denied the right to live the life he believes in, he has no choice but to become an outlaw'. Criminal cases have always been popular in the news and media as well as among novelists & filmmakers etc. There are several reasons behind a person committing crime. Poverty, lack of proper education, alcohol and substance abuse, low self-esteem etc. are just a few reasons among a whole lot. Theft, robbery, rape, murder, kidnapping, abduction etc. are the types of crime that is commonly seen to be committed in our society. Our societal set up and crime against women enable us to think: Do women get justice? In terms of her work, sacrifices, makers of family, society and the nation, it is felt that there is gross-injustice to their end. It can be seen looking at their crimes and violence that they faced or facing. The present work emphasis on women pertaining to history and development of crimes against women in the Indian context, critical interpretation of various legislations and possible changes for the benefit of women. Doctrinal method and journals, books, web resources are used to prepare the narrative.

Crime against women is of different nature. There are reports on domestic violence happened between people in an intimate relationship. It again multiplied into physical, sexual, verbal & emotional and economic. Physical violence includes assault, criminal intimidation and criminal force. Sexual violence refers any conduct of a sexual nature that humiliates and degrades the dignity of a woman. Verbal and emotional violence include insults, humiliation or ridicule for not having a child or male child and threats to cause harm to any person in whom the aggrieved person is interested. An abuser may restrict their partner from acquiring, using and making money and economic resources such as food, clothing, transportation etc. This behavior is known as economic abuse. Another sort of crimes like rape and murder is found increasing in India, acid attack (most of cases due to refusal of marriage proposal or rejection of love), sexual harassment in workplace and marital rape. Marital rape literally denotes when there is forceful biological relation without the consent of wife. However, Indian society has given more importance to rape whereas the act of marital rape didn't get the required attention yet. Earlier there is another sort of injustice to women where there is female feticide due to aspiration of son. It is cut short by legislations making predetermination of sex as crime. In some societies, there is report of child marriage. Woman of the few parts of the country including north east, faces injustice when they are pushed to death in the name of witch hunting.

Present India is the reflection of the past in case of woman. They are humiliated in the past and even at present. India's world view is not reflected in its' reality. There is female goddess whom is worshipped since time immemorial. At the same time, women had hard realities. In ancient times, most of the Raja's and Maharaja's used to have 3-4 wives and they used to marry when their first wife dies. But, on the other hand, when the husband dies, the wife is declared as widow and she was not allowed to wear any colorful attire. She also had to cut her hair, she was not allowed to eat non-vegetarian food. There was another ritual in the ancient times that if the husband dies, the wife would have to or was forced to jump into the funeral pyre of her husband. This was known as *sati dah* tradition. Besides girls were not encouraged to go to school and get education. Society has stereotypic vision and considered girls were born to do household chores and hence they were not allowed to do other work. But there were some role models like Rani Laxmi Bai, Razia Sultan, Ahilya Bai Holkar etc. who created history by their works. Rani Laxmi Bai was married to Gangdhar of Jhansi. When both her husband and son died, she adopted a child to make him the heir of the throne. But British Governor Dalhousie refused to recognize the adoption and ordered to annexed Jhansi. Rani Laxmi Bai joined other rulers and started rebelling against British rule. Though she was not successful to save her life and the throne but she created history, as at that time a woman fighting against men was never seen ever before. There were other women Razia Sultana who ruled Delhi Sultanate. This is how women created history from time to time but men somewhere suppressed them. After the annexation of India by the British, there were certain changes that took place. They tried to change our ancient culture and banned certain old rituals. The most famous ritual of ancient India - sati tradition was banned by Lord William Bentrick in the year 1829. They also promoted remarriage of Hindu widow, abolished infanticides, etc. In the midst of adverse situation, some noted personality came forward to work for the benefit of woman. They were - Raja Ram Mohan Roy, Swami Vivekananda, Lala Lajpat Rai, Bal Gangadhar Tilak, Bipin Chandra Pal, Ishwarchandra Vidyasagar, etc. Peary Charan Sarkar, a former student of Hindu College Culcutta, set up the first free school for girls in India in 1847. Ishwarchandra Vidyasagar also worked for the improvement in the situation of widows. Slowly, some changes took place in our society. Women are now allowed to attend school and take higher education. Still there are some places in India where women are considered as slave. Women are still not getting the freedom.

Though sati regulation, child marriage, etc. have been abolished, still in some places women are being raped, murdered for dowry, need to live the life of a widow after her husbands' death. These are still prevailing in our society. In the past there were attempts to provide justice for woman. But in contemporary times, opposite pictures prevails when we examine the Indian situation in recent times.

According to a poll of 2011 conduct by the Thomson Reuters foundation, India is the 4th most dangerous country in the world for women. According to a research of 2011, the age group of below 18 years tends to commit rape while criminals with their ages between 18-30 years tend to insult the modesty of women, kidnap and rape them. The age group of 30-60 years tends to be arrested for the crimes of cruelty by husband or his relatives. NCRB data for 2018 pegged U.P. as the most unsafe for women while Madhya Pradesh recorded the most number of rape cases. According to a statistical data, U.P. registered 59,445 cases of crime against women; Madhya Pradesh registered 5,450 rape cases, the maximum in 2018. In total, 3,78,277 cases of crimes against women were reported across the country in 2018. The record also shows that domestic violence against women figures as the top category of violence against women in 2018.

Legislation has takes noteworthy step to provide justice to the woman since colonial days. During British rule, many acts were passed including Bengal Sati Regulation 1829, Hindu Widow Remarriage Act 1856, Female Infanticide Prevention Act 1870 and Age of Consent Act 1891. In 1917, the first women's delegation met the Secretary of State to demand women's political rights, supported by Indian National Congress. The All India Women's Education Conference was held in Pune in 1927, which became a major organization forsocial change. In the year 1929, the Child Marriage Restraint Act was passed. After the adoption of the Indian Constitution, it guaranteed to all equality to all under Article 14, no discrimination by the state Art 15(1), equality of opportunity Art 16, equal pay for equal work Art 39(d) & Art 42. In addition to that special provision to be made by the State in favor of women and children Art 15(3), resources practices derogatory to the dignity for women Art 51(A)(e), securing just and humane conditions of work and for maternity relief under Art 42.

Feminism in India gained importance in the late 70's. One of the first national level issues was the 'Mathura Rape Case'. The acquittal of policemen accused of raping a young girl from Mathura in a police station led to a countrywide protest in 1974-80. The protest forced the Indian Government to amend the Evidence Act, CrPC and IPC and created a new offence 'custodial rape'. In the 1990's many NGO's were formed which played a major role in the advancement of women's rights in India. Judiciary's interventions also play some important role in fetching justice for women pertaining to executing religious rights. In 1991, Kerela High Court restricted the entry of women above the age of 10 and below the age of 50 from 'Sabarimala' as they were of the menstruating age. However, on 28th September 2018, the Supreme Court of India lifted the ban on the entry of women.

Indian legislation has always making attempt to provide safeguard for woman in the last three or four decades or so. The National Policy for Empowerment of Women was passed in 2001. In 2005, Parliament enacted the special statute to be known as the Protection of women from domestic violence Act, 2005. This is an act to provide for more effective protection of the rights of women guaranteed under the Constitution of India, who are victims of any kind, occurring within the family and for matters connected therewith. The Pre-natal Diagnostics Techniques Act, 1994 was enacted to prohibit sex selection techniques. In order to extend illegal abortions, the Medical termination of Pregnancy Act, 1971 has been enacted. Our Parliament enacted the Dowry Prohibition Act, 1961 to prohibit the giving and taking of dowry. But in spite of this enactment, dowry still prevails in our country. On 9th March 2010, Rajya Sabha passed the Women's Reservation Bill acquiring that 33 % seats in Parliament and State Legislature will be reserved for women. The Sexual Harassment of Women at workplace (Prevention,

Prohibition & Redressal) Act 2013 is a legislative act in India that seeks to protect women from sexual harassment at their workplace. The Criminal Law (Amendment) Act, 2013 introduced changes to the Indian Penal Code, making sexual harassment as an expressed offence under Sec 354 A, which is punishable up to 3 years of imprisonment and/or with fine. The Amendment also introduced new sections making acts like disrobing a woman without consent; stalking and sexual an act by person is an offence. It also made acid attacks a specific offence with imprisonment for not less than 10 years, which could extend to life imprisonment and with fine.

On 22nd August 2017, the Indian Supreme Court declared triple talaq as unconstitutional. Our Government has also constituted some schemes for women such as Beti Bachao, Beti Parhao, Ujjawala, etc. which has shown a ray of hope for the improvement of the state of women.

Though our Constitution and government have taken various steps to eliminate crimes against women, and there overall improvement there is a lot of things that need to addressed. India has travelled a lot in its fight against crime on women but there is still a lot of work to be done, especially in the Indian villages where the crime against women is at the peak, besides rural women suffering at the hands of violence at a domestic level also. So government should arrange some public awareness program for remote areas. So that the laws and procedures could reach to the women of those rural places and they could stand for their rights and raise their voice against crime. In India most of the crimes against women are unreported because of social stigma attached to it as well as fear. Moreover, conviction rate is very low, long trials and continuous insult to the victim prevent many women to speak up. Therefore, government should create an atmosphere where more females come out seeking justice for wrong doings to her. Time taken by our judiciary system to solve such cases takes more that a year or may be more than that to come to a conclusion. Where as there is an option of fast track court, so all these women related criminal cases should be handled by them. So that there is no delay in justice as justice delayed is justice denied. Our laws must be strict so that no one dares to commit a crime. Government should introduce and should make it compulsory for girls to undergo self-defense training classes in schools and colleges. Government should give more opportunities to women in services and in business dealing etc. to improve their status. Government should increase patrolling duties of policemen in public places, especially during dark hours. Man is not the only one who is violent against women. Women are also violent against other women. It is the mother-in-law who starts violence against their daughter-in-law. They look at their daughter and their daughter-in-law in two very different perspectives. Hence, it is the need of the hour for women to change their attitude towards other fellow women.

Violence and crime against women has become a global phenomenon. Every woman deserves a fear free and respectable life. And it is our responsibility to create such a society where a woman is able to live with dignity and respect. And we can firmly say, yes, 'women will get justice.'

SELECTED READINGS AND WEB SOURCES

1. Legal Language Legal Writing by Dr. S.C. Tripathi
2. Introduction to Constitution of India by Durga Das Basu
3. Hindu Law by R.K. Agarwal
4. www.legalservisecindia.com
5. www.washingtonpost.com
6. www.ncrb.gov.in
7. www.jstor.org
8. www.unicef.inc.org
9. www.thehindu.com

9

Marital Rape in India: The Ugly Truth behind Closed Doors

Soyonika Gogoi

Marriage is an institution which binds two people in a bond of lifetime. Love and respect are the two most important pillars in a relationship; however, sadly this is not the case always. Rape is an offence of unlawful sex committed by a man on a woman by using force which is punishable under the Indian Penal Code, 1860 but surprisingly marital rape which is a concept of commission of sex by spouse with his better half without her consent is not covered within the ambit of the IPC, 1860 for conviction. Marital rape is not considered an offence in India and the existing patriarchal system in the country plays a huge role in the continuing ordeal. Rape is not only savagery against ladies but rather a grave infringement of a person's basic ideal to life and individual freedom. In this manner it is not right to trust that sex with spouse is husband's privilege given to him by marriage. Today numerous nations have either established marital rape laws, revoked marital rape special cases or have laws that do not recognize marital rape and ordinary rape. This demonstrates marital rape is currently perceived as an infringement of human rights. Marital rape in India is viewed as rape only if the wife is under 15 years of age and the punishment for such offence is also milder. There is no lawful security agreed to the spouse after the age of 15, which is against human rights directions. Most of arguments propounded for non criminalisation of marital rape in India includes the argument of adequate legal remedies such as protection under Section 498-A under IPC and the Protection of Women under the Domestic Violence Act, 2005.

This endeavour seeks to understand the ugly truth of marital rape in India and arguments regarding why marital rape should be criminalised and why it should not be criminalised in India. The concept of marital rape has been a topic of debate from ever since and it is high time that India enacts a new law for criminalisation of marital rape for giving protection to victims above 15 years of age. The existing laws do not discuss about marital rape *per se* and treats marital rape as a type of local violence.[1] To provide legal protection to victims of such an offence the legislature and judiciary must step into the shoes of the victims and criminalising such acts can bring a fear in the minds of the accused who will think twice before committing such an offence.

INTRODUCTION

Rape derived from the Latin term "rapine" or "rapere" is an offence against a woman which is committed by a man against her will and without her consent. The Latin terms referred to the more general violations - looting, destruction, enslavement, taking away and capture of citizens - inflicted upon a tribe, town, city or country during war. Sexual connotation associated with it came much later.[2] It is defined under Section 375 of the Indian Penal Code, 1860 (hereinafter referred as IPC, 1860) and includes all forms of sexual assault involving non consensual intercourse with a woman.[3] It is an offence against a woman violating her dignity and self respect and is punishable under Section 376 IPC, 1860 with imprisonment of either description for a term which shall not be less than seven years but which may extend to 10 years and shall also be liable to fine. However, the irony of this concept is that when it occurs within the four walls of a matrimonial home it is not considered an offence, despite the fact that it reduces the woman to the status of an object used merely for sexual gratification. Marital rape committed by a husband has never been a subject of rape laws.

Laws bestowed an absolute immunity on the husband in respect of his wife, solely on the basis of marital relation. The revolution started with women activists in America during the women's movement in 1970s. The revolution helped in increasing the sensitivity of the women and society towards two major crimes namely sexual assault and physical assault by their husbands which women usually fall victim. Victims of rape and wives who are sexually assaulted by their own husbands share a great deal in common. Both these crimes have been the most underreported crimes against persons in the criminal justice system. In most cases of the rape or physical assault cases by husbands, women who turn to the criminal justice system for assistance or relief are often maltreated or ignored by police, lawyers, and judges.[4] The revolution was a mere attempt for elimination of marital rare exemption clause and extension of guarantee of equal protection to women. However, keeping in mind the scenario that still exists in India there is an immediate need for a distinct law on marital or spousal rape in India, which should be at par with the accepted international norms on this issue.

THE UGLY TRUTH OF MARITAL RAPE IN INDIA

Marital rape or spousal rape can be generally defined as unwanted intercourse obtained by a woman's husband or ex-husband through force, or when she is unable to consent.[5] A woman marries with the desire of commitment, love and care. But imagine a scenario where on the very first night of her marriage instead of love and respect she is portrayed as a commodity with no wish of her own by her husband is an utter nightmare for every person. The trauma does not stop here, moreover, it continues to the point of being compelled to enact pornographic material to that of insertion of objects into her vagina. Now imagine the condition of the woman who suffers this every night of her married life and when she finally gathers the courage to speak of it to her family members she is hushed by them stating not to bring on the table about her bedroom affairs. If she approaches the police she is asked to be grateful to her husband as he is being faithful to her. What does she do then because standing for her rights in such a case is not welcomed in the society we live in. The law of land does not itself consider marital rape as a crime and non criminalization of this unfortunate reality threatens the life of countless married women in our country.

The lack of laws and abundant social stigmas against the act of marital rape is one of the primary reasons that are still hidden behind the veil of marriage. The woman has been given the right to fight for protection when the violators are outside entities, but when the perpetrator of her bodily integrity is her own husband; such protection is withdrawn by the legislators. This idea is absolutely unacceptable to a civilized society. Therefore there is no justification or applicability of the notion of marital exemption in the current times. It is true that mere criminalization of marital rape in India will not end the problem, but it is sure an important step towards changing women's experience of sexual violence in a marriage. It is high time that the concept of "rape is rape, irrespective of the relationship between the victim and the perpetrator" is recognized by the law and put strictly to force.

STATISTICAL STUDY OF MARITAL RAPE IN INDIA

Marital rape is currently underreported because of cultural norms, social stigma, and the fact that many countries lack a supportive justice system and India is one of such countries.[6] As per the latest National Family Health Survey-4 National Report, 2015-16 (NFHS-4) which receives technical guidance from the Ministry of Health and Family Welfare reports 31% of the married women (nearly one in three) have been subjugated to physical, sexual and emotional violence at the hands of their spouse. The number has reduced from 37% in 2005- 06 to 29% in 2015-16. Despite the reduction in number there continues to be a lot of cases of married women suffering physical and sexual violence at the hands of their husbands.[7] The survey also states that 83% of married women between the ages of 15 to 49 years have cited their current husband as the perpetrator while 7% of the women have stated their former spouse as the perpetrator. The NFHS-4 data states that only 14% of abused women seek external assistance when subjected to violence by husband which is reportedly less compared to the previous survey of 24% conducted by NFHS.

Another study conducted by the United Nations Population Fund (UNPFA) estimated that over 40 percent of married women in India between the age group of 15 to 49 years of age have been beaten, raped or forced to engage in sexual intercourse with their spouses.[8]

In 2011 a Washington based non-profit organization named the International Centre for Research on women during the survey conducted found out that one in every five men in

India have admitted to forcing their wives for sexual intercourse. The survey also disclosed the fact that only one in four abused women speak up about such acts and seek for help. Moreover, it was also clear from the survey that women are more likely to seek help for physical violence rather than for sexual violence. When such violation occurs women typically approach family members rather than the police.[9]

Sadly the ordeal still continues and despite the huge number of surveys revealing the displeasing truth about such forced sexual intercourse by the spouse there are cases as per the NFHS-4 report that 42% of men and 52% of women believe that husbands are justified in unleashing violence on women, including if the wife refuses to engage in sexual intercourse.

This shows how the issue is not merely about bringing into force a law to criminalise it but also about changing the mindsets.[10]

MARITAL RAPE NOT CONSIDERED RAPE IN INDIA

It has been an uphill struggle for women's movements in India to make marital rape the most important topic for discussion. Not surprisingly enough there has been very little or no legal support to the idea of rape within the institution of marriage. This absence has been compounded by social attitudes that refuse to accept that there could be lack of consent within marriage. The legality of marriage has been founded on the act of "consummation", while the inability to have sex provides grounds for its annulment. Most importantly, the husband has the right to demand "restitution of conjugal rights" or take the support of the State to get sexual access to his wife who may be unwillingly to participate in sexual relations. The question that comes up in this context is what would be the definition of marital rape be in the cases where the consent of the women to marriage is taken for granted. While some argue that in a country like India criminalising marital rape has the potential to disturb the organisation of the contemporary Indian family, others argue that criminalising marital rape is essential to any politics which foregrounds democratisation of gender relations.[11]

Advancing well into the timeline, as per a research by United Nations marital rape has been criminalized in four countries out of 10 countries. The *World's Women Report* states that a dozen of countries allow rapists to avoid prosecution by marrying their victims. From Iraq to Malaysia, women are ramping up pressure to abolish marry-your-rapist laws after Tunisia, Jordan and Lebanon scrapped similar articles in 2017. Marital rape has been criminalized in more than 50 countries including United States, Nepal and South Africa, however, the case is not same in most of Asia, where campaigners are pushing for legal reform.[12] Despite amendments, law commissions and new legislations, one of the most humiliating and debilitating acts is not an offence in India. A look at the options a woman has to protect herself in a marriage tells us that the legislations have been either non-existent or obscure and everything has just depended on the interpretation by the courts.

In the wake of the brutal gang rape of a 23 year old woman in 2012, India strengthened its sexual assault legislation. But despite calls from activists, a man who rapes his wife cannot be punished under the Indian laws. Section 375, the provision of rape in the Indian Penal Code, 1860 has been echoing very archaic sentiments, mentioned as its exception clause- "Sexual intercourse by man with his own wife, the wife not being under 15 years of age, is not rape."[13] In a recent case of PILs being filed by RIT Foundation and the All India Democratic Women's Association challenging the constitutionality of Section 375 (which defines rape) and to strike down the exception in the Indian penal law that does not consider sexual intercourse with a wife, not less than 15 years of age, as rape. The petitions have also sought setting aside of the exception in the rape law that protects husbands, saying that it violates the right to equality, freedom and to live life with dignity provided under the Constitution. The Delhi High Court stated that:

> "Marriage does not mean that the woman is all time ready, willing and consenting (for establishing physical relations). The man will have to prove that she was a consenting party."

It did not agree with the submission of NGO Men Welfare Trust, which is opposed the plea to make marital rape an offence, that in spousal sexual violence, the use of force or threat of force are important elements to constitute the offence.[14] Section 376 of IPC provided punishment for rape. According to the section, the rapist should be punished with imprisonment of either description for a term which shall not be less than 7 years but which may extend to life or for a term extending up to 10 years and shall also be liable to fine unless the woman raped is his own wife and is not under 12 years of age, in which case, he shall be punished with imprisonment of either description for a term which may extend to 2 years with fine or with both.[15] This section in dealing with sexual assault, in a very narrow purview lays down that an offence of rape within marital bonds stands only if the wife is less than 12 years of age, if she is between 12 to 16 years, an offence is committed, however, less serious, attracting milder punishment. Once, the age crosses 16 years there is no legal protection accorded to the wife in direct contravention of human rights regulations.

How can the same law provide for the legal age of consent for marriage to be 18 years while protecting from sexual abuse only to the age of 16 years? Beyond the age of 16 years there is no remedy which can be claimed by the woman. A marriage is a bond of trust and affection. A husband exercising sexual superiority by getting it on demand and through any means possible is not part of the institution. Surprisingly, this is not, as yet in any law book in India.

The very definition of rape in the IPC 1860 demands change. The narrow definition has been criticized by the Indian and international women's and children's organizations, who insists that acts including oral sex, sodomy and penetration by foreign objects within the meaning of rape would not have been inconsistent with any constitutional provisions, natural justice or equity.

Criminalizing marital rape was also among the suggestions of the Late Justice J.S Verma Committee, a three-member panel appointed to suggest amendments to India's sexual assault laws. The government rejected this proposed change, leaving it out of the draft bill presented before the Parliament.[16] According to the report submitted to the Parliament a panel of lawmakers who opposed the move argued it has the potential of destroying the institution of marriage. The report further added "If marital rape is brought under the law, the entire family system will be under great stress". Lawyers and women's rights activists have sharply criticized the decision to leave marital rape out of the penal code. The act of rape itself destroys the institution of marriage, not the ability or inability to legally prosecute such an offence. Rape is rape and there are no exceptions to it. These statements defeat the entire purpose of the bill itself as well as deny a married woman the fundamental right to protect herself from non-consensual sex.

ARGUMENTS SUPPORTING CRIMINALISATION OF MARITAL RAPE IN INDIA

There have been arguments both for and against the idea of criminalisation of marital rape in India. Exemption of marital rape as a crime in India contravenes both the constitutional as well as international obligations. Since our country has been progressing in every sector of development, the justifications for the existence of an archaic law reflects the old and outdated approach of our society.

a. ***Contravention with the Constitution of India*** - Article 13, of the Indian Constitution states that any law in force if in contravention with any if the fundamental rights of an individual shall be void.[17] It can be stated that Article 13 is directly hit by the exception of the marital rape under IPC as it violates some of the very basic fundamental rights guaranteed to an individual. Article 14 of the Indian Constitution states that the state provides to all equality before law and equal protection of law. While the phrase "equality before law" ensures that all person shall be treated equally without any special privileges to any of them, the phrase "equal protection of law" ensures the concept of positive discrimination and that there should be equality amongst equal and not unequal. Thus creating the concept of positive discrimination. The marital exception clause fails to fulfil this test of reasonable classification as provided under article 14 and article 15(3), which should be based on intelligible differentia and reasonable nexus.[18]

   Moreover, Article 21 provides that every individual has the right to life and the right to personal liberty, which includes within it a life comprising of something more than mere animal existence and a life of dignity.[19]

Therefore, allowing the marital rape clause under the statute thus directly infringes a person's right to live with dignity and honour. Supreme Court in a variety of cases has stated that Article 21 includes woman's right to bodily integrity and her right to privacy and that she is entitled to the protection of law in case of intrusion.[20] Additionally, the Supreme Court of India has interpreted article 21 to comprise of right to health and the offence of rape is known to consist of a plethora of physical as well as psychological problems thus violating the right under article 21 for married women.[21]

b. ***Contravention with Obligations under International Law*** - Marital rape has been declared illegal in 18 American States, 3 Australian States, New Zealand, Canada, Israel, France, Sweden, Denmark, Norway, Soviet Union, Poland and Czechoslovakia. Rape in any form is considered an utter humiliation, degradation and violation rather than any outdated concept of penile/vaginal penetration. Restricting an understanding of rape reaffirms the view that rapists treat rape as sex and no violence and hence, condone such behaviour.[22] Even the United Nations Convention on the Elimination of All Forms of Discrimination against Women (CEDAW), of which India is a signatory, has viewed that this sort of discrimination against women violates the principles of equality of rights and respect for human dignity. Further, the Commission on Human Rights, at its fifty-first session, in its Resolution No. 1995/85 of 8-3-1995 titled "The elimination of violence against women", recommended that marital rape should be criminalized.[23] Article 2 (a) of the Declaration of the Elimination of Violence against Women includes marital rape explicitly in the definition of violence against women.[24] Emphasis on these provisions is meant to give the victim and not the criminal, the benefit of doubt. The United Nations General Assembly through its Resolution 71/170 too called upon the member states to implement and take effective steps towards violence relating to marital rape.[25] Maintaining the marital rape exemption violates the provisions of the CEDAW as it requires the state parties to eliminate prejudices that perpetuate stereotypes on the basis of gender and the act of marital rape leads to a portrayal of women as sexual property thus denying her equal status in the family. Lastly penalising marital rape would lead to fulfilling India's obligation under the UDHR and the ICESCR to protect an individual's right to health and well-being.

ARGUMENTS AGAINST CRIMINALISATION OF MARITAL RAPE IN INDIA

Though our country has advanced in all possible fields, marital rape is still not considered as an offence in India. One cannot criminalize marital rape unless supplemented with amendments in the Hindu Marriage Act. But amending laws related to Hinduism is near to impossible given the frail religious sentiments in the country. The arguments which stand against criminalisation of marital rape in India are: The theory of implied consent, the recourse of legal protection by abused wives, role of Indian culture and misuse of the law.

a. **Theory of Implied Consent** - The origin of the marital rape exemption can be traced back to statements by Sir Mathew Hale, Chief Justice of England, during 1736. He wrote, "The husband cannot be guilty of a rape committed by himself upon his lawful wife, for by their mutual matrimonial consent and contract the wife hath given up herself in this kind unto her husband, which she cannot retract."[26] According to him a marriage is a contract and a woman impliedly consents to sexual intercourse. In India it is not new to say that freedom of women after marriage lies at the hands of their husbands. Thus the argument that marriage implies consent is still used in justifying marital rape as seen by the Law Commission of India's 172nd Report on Review of Rape Laws of 2000.[27]

b. **Recourse to other legal protection** – One of the most common arguments put forward against the idea of having a proper law for criminalising marital rape accused persons in India is that there are adequate legal remedies available to the victims such as legal provisions under the Protection of Women from Violence Act, Section 498A of the Indian Penal Code and various other personal laws dealing with divorce and marriage. However, the much awaited Domestic Violence Act, 2005 (DVA) has also been a disappointment. It has provided civil remedies to what the provision of cruelty already gave criminal remedies, while keeping the status of the matter of marital rape in continuing disregard. It condones sexual abuse in a domestic relationship of marriage or a live-in, only if it is life threatening or grievously hurtful. It is not about the freedom of decision of a woman's wants.[28] Victims had recourse to Section 498-A which deals with cruelty, to protect themselves against "perverse sexual conduct by the husband".[29] The Hindu Marriage Act provides "cruelty" as a ground for divorce. None of the above mentioned remedies do anything to deter the violent behaviour of the husbands but only provide for a way out for the wife or grant her a civil remedy. The Supreme Court in India upheld that denial of conjugal relations may amount to cruelty and thus can be a ground for divorce.[30] Therefore; it becomes more practical to criminalise marital rape and retain the recourse for men to apply for divorce on denial of sexual relations as cruelty.

c. **Role of Indian Culture** - Our Indian cultural plays a major role in non criminalisation of marital rape. According to traditional Hindu beliefs denying of sex goes against the duties of an ideal wife. It is common for a court to grant divorce on the grounds that a wife denies her husband sexual intercourse. The cultural construct of marriage as a sacred and pious relationship and any criminal intrusion into it would destabilize its foundation.[31] This argument has been turned down by the Supreme Court stating that marriage is a personal affair and the state has no role in destabilizing it. The court further held that if the presence of legal remedies like divorce and judicial separation could not be seen as destroying the institution of marriage criminalising marital rape too could not be seen as an instrument to destabilise the institution of marriage. On the other hand acts of marital rape damage the institution of marriage which is based on trust and confidence and thus it is the duty of the state to protect the constitutional rights of the individuals within this institution.[32]

d. **Misuse of new Law** – Most of the arguments based on the reason for not having a law for criminalising marital rape in India is that there are chances of misusing the law against the innocents. Similar arguments have been raised in the past against some of the other laws enacted for the protection of women in spite of their failure to provide any empirical data on the same.

CONCLUSION

Marital Rape is not a newly built concept. It has always been a part of our society but has been considered as a taboo when talked about. It is time that we come out and speak about it openly so that such acts which exist behind closed doors come to a halt at the earliest. It is important to understand that marriage does not thrive on sex and the fear of frivolous litigation should not stop protection from being offered to those caught in abusive traps, where they are denigrated to the status of chattel. In this era legal reforms and revolutions it is of utmost importance that laws for criminalising marital rape should be brought up. Apart from judicial awakening; we primarily require generation of awareness. Men are the perpetrators of this crime. 'Educating boys and men to view women as valuable partners in life, in the development of society and the attainment of peace are just as important as taking legal steps protect women's human rights', says the UN. Men have the social, economic, moral, political, religious and social responsibility to combat all forms of gender discrimination. In a country rife with misconceptions of rape, deeply ingrained cultural and religious stereotypes, and changing social values, globalization has to fast alter the letter of law.

"CONSENT IS CONSENT
NO IS NO
RAPE IS RAPE"

END NOTES

1. Sanghamitra Loganathan, *"Marital Rape"*, LSI, available at http://www.legalservicesindia.com/article/2369/Marital-Rape.html (accessed on 19.07.2020)
2. Stellina Jolly and M.S. Raste, *"Rape and Marriage: Reflections on the Past, Present and Future"*, 48 JILI 279 (2006).

3. Sarthak Makkar, *"Marital Rape – A non criminalized crime in India",* HHRJ, Jan 1, 2019, available at https://harvardhrj.com/2019/01/marital-rape-a-non-criminalized-crime-in-india/
4. Richard J. Gelles, *"Power, Sex, and Violence: The Case of Marital Rape",* TFL, Oct.1977, Vol. 26, No. 4, available at *JSTOR*, www.jstor.org/stable/581754. Accessed 16 July 2020
5. Lance Gable et.al. *"Legal aspects of HIV/AIDS :A guide for Policy and Legal Reform",* Global HIV/AIDS Program and Legal Vice Presidency, The World Bank
6. LANCE GABLE ET.AL, Supra *note* 2
7. Rinchen Norbhu Wangchuk, *"Survey takes veil off marital rape in India: It's time we had a serious discussion",* The Better India, Mar 16, 2018, available at https://www.thebetterindia.com/134673/survey-nfhs- marital-rape-india/
8. Neeta Lal, *"The definition of rape cannot change with a Marriage certificate",* IPS, July 14 2020, available at http://www.ipsnews.net/2015/05/the-definition-of-rape-cannot-change-with-a-marriage-certificate/

9 *Ibid*

10. Rinchen norbhu wangchuk, *Supra Note* 4

11 *"Marriage and Rape: We Need a Law on Marital Rape but Such Acts Cannot Be Separated from the Structure of the Indian Family."* Economic and Political Weekly 48, no. 12 (2013): 7-8. [accessed July 16, 2020], available at www.jstor.org/stable/23527135.

12. Ellen Wulfhorst, *"UN Urges Countries to End Marital Rape and Close Legal Loopholes",* Global citizen, 26 June, 2019, available at: https://www.globalcitizen.org/en/content/un-women-marital-rape-laws/, [accessed 17 July 2020
13. Section 375, IPC, 1860, Act No.45 of 1860 (6th Oct 1860)
14. PTI, *"Delhi HC on marital rape: Marriage doesn't mean wife always ready for physical relations with her husband",* Published: July 18, 2018 11:53 AM, available at https://www.financialexpress.com/india- news/delhi-hc-on-marital-rape-marriage-doesnt-mean-wife-always-ready-for-physical-relations-with-her- husband/1248987/
15. Section 376, IPC, 1860, Act No.45 of 1860 (6th Oct 1860)
16. Krina Patel, *"The Gap in Marital Rape Law in India: Advocating for Criminalization and Social Change",* 42 FILJ 1525 (2019)
17. The Indian Const. 1950, Art. 13
18. Ruchita Kaundal, *"Marital Rape in India: Need for Criminalization",* WBLJ, Vol.2, Issue 1, May 2020

19. Bandhua Mukti Morcha v. Union of India *AIR 1984 SC 802*
20. State of Maharashtra v. Madhukar Narayan Mardikar *AIR 1991 SC 207*, also see Suchita Srivastava & Anr vs Chandigarh Administration (2009) 14 SCR 989
21. MAKKAR, *Supra* note 2
22. Priyanka Rath, *"Marital Rape and the Indian legal scenario"*, ILJ, Vol. II Issue 2, available at https://www.indialawjournal.org/archives/volume2/issue_2/article_by_priyanka.html
23. Aishwarya Mishra, *"India: Law On Marital Rape – A Much Needed Reform In Our Legal System"*, Mondaq, 13 April 2018, available at https://www.mondaq.com/india/crime/691482/law-on-marital-rape-a-much-needed- reform-in-our-legal-system
24. Declaration on the Elimination of Violence against Women, Proclaimed by General Assembly resolution 48/104 of 20 December 1993
25. KAUNDAL, *Supra* note 18
26. M. V. Sankaran, *"The Marital Status Exemption in Rape"*, 20 JILI 597 (1978)
27. Law Commission of India, 172nd Report on Review of Rape Laws (March, 2000), available at: http://www.lawcommissionofindia.nic.in/rapelaws.htm#chapter3, [accessed on 19-07-2020
28. RATH, *Supra* note 21
29. The Indian Penal Code,1860, Section 498A
30. Editorial, "Denial of sex by spouse is cruelty: Supreme Court ", The Time of India, Sep. 26, 2014. (accessed 19.07.2020)
31. RATH, *Supra* note 21
32. *Ibid.*

10

Violence against Women: India and the World

Suhavi Arya

INTRODUCTION

Violence against women is a much-reported topic right now but it has been going on since time immemorial. The violence which used to be state-sponsored, where husbands (even in European households) were legally allowed to impose "moderate correction", if necessary[1] has now changed in several aspects. It has deep-seated roots in our history. The roots of which stem from ancient notions of patriarchy that were first introduced to the rest of the world by the Bible, where Eve was made from the rib of Adam which reinforces a woman's inferiority. Dr. Fox argues that it was rise of militarism which led to establishment of patriarchy and male dominance: women fell into the group of being dominated, because of their inferior strength and nurturing personalities[2]. It was later reinforced via common law, where women are often treated as a property, by first their father, brother and then their husbands.[3]

Since given the right to vote, women all over the world are slowly, but surely realising their rights. Several different brands of feminism have been spoken about, while some have derailed, there is a quiet realisation, that the main concept of women being equal to men and being given equal treatment and rights, is here to stay. Several countries are dealing with these new waves in their own ways. In India, there is an added problem of illiteracy, population, economic issues, along with societal evils such as the caste system which, along with patriarchy play a major role at how women are viewed, how violence is instigated and the kind of attempts being made on curbing such violence. This endeavour will aim to address how international bodies and India are addressing violence against women. It will also look into how violence against women is recognized in conflicts (in the Rome Statute) as it is important to recognize the different experiences.

HISTORY OF VIOLENCE AGAINST WOMEN: THE INTERNATIONAL PERSPECTIVE

United Nations has adopted several treaties to eliminate violence against women, the most important one being Convention on the Elimination of all Forms of Discrimination Against Women (CEDAW), which is based on three main principles: "the obligation to respect (equality in laws and policies); the obligation to protect (non-discrimination–direct and indirect) and the obligation fulfil (to uphold equality and eliminate gender discrimination in the entire sphere of the social and economic life)".[4]

Moreover, several General Recommendations,[5] recommended by the Committee on the Elimination of all Forms of Discrimination against Women, but especially Recommendations

12[6] and 14[7] have further strengthened this initiative. It should be noted that the India ratified[8] CEDAW in 1993.

The UN General Assembly in its 1993[9] declaration on the Elimination of violence against women stated that violence against women can be defined as "any act of gender-based violence that results in, or is likely to result in, physical, sexual or psychological harm or suffering to women, including threats of such acts, coercion or arbitrary deprivation of liberty, whether occurring in public or in private life". It went on to establish a sub-organ within itself to focus on women's rights (including curbing violence against women): UN Women[10] in 2011. 25th November[11] is also celebrated as International Day for the Elimination of Violence against Women. In fact, an inter-governmental body, established in 1946, known as the Commission on the Status of Women[12] was also set up, which also looks at among other things, implementing international framework on curbing violence against women. Goal 5 of Sustainable Development Goals also calls for 'Gender equality', where the aim is to systematically work towards giving the same rights to women as men, while curbing sexual violence[13]. One may wonder that this is 2020, it's the 21st century, we should be way past such discussions, but, globally, these figures are alarming:

- "1 in 3 women and girls experience physical or sexual violence in their lifetime, most frequently by an intimate partner …
- Worldwide, almost 750 million women and girls alive today were married before their 18th birthday; while 200 million women and girls have undergone female genital mutilation (FGM)
- 1 in 2 women killed worldwide were killed by their partners or family in 2017; while only 1 out of 20 men were killed under similar circumstances…"[14]

According to UN Women estimates "35% of women in the world have experienced either physical and/or sexual intimate partner violence or sexual violence by a non-partner (not including sexual harassment) at some point in their lives".[15] While some studies show that approximately 70% women of some countries have experienced the same.[16] Although the numbers are high, they still don't reflect the differences between urban and rural areas of Global North and the Global South. The situation is completely different conflict zones.

LAWS ON VIOLENCE AGAINST WOMEN IN (INTERNATIONAL) CONFLICT ZONES

Violence against women has been used as tool in conflict zones. It is not a new phenomenon. There are several incidents in history, however, since the present day concepts of international law were mainly developed in the 20th century, so did the conversation around sexual violence in times of peace and war. Universal Declaration of Human Rights (UDHR) was one of the first such global document that recognized several 'universal' rights for all human beings. It enshrines right to life, liberty and security of person. At the same time, international criminal law was also being developed, because World War II had just ended but then the Charter of the Nuremberg Trials, that was agreed upon, in 1945 (the same year), it did not include rape as a provision to indict any of the accused. This was in direct violation of 'right to security of person' enshrined by the UDHR. This was because there wasn't enough political will. The main opposition for the same were the Soviets who had used rape and other forms of sexual violence against Germans in Berlin in the last leg of the war.[17] Over the years crimes of sexual violence were mostly dealt with under crimes of honour and dignity, like in the Geneva Conventions. The Security Council, while establishing the ICTY in 1993, restricted the sexual violence provisions to only rape, negating other forms of sexual violence. It was prescribed under Crimes against Humanity. Conversely, the cases before the ICTY and ICTR shocked the conscience of the world and created a space for jurisprudence on sexual and gender issues. The conviction of genocide,[18] on the basis of evidence from sexual crimes was a huge step forward in the direction of recognizing and criminalizing gender and sexual violence in international law. International conferences,[19] United Nations[20] condemning violence on the basis of sex lead to the inclusion of sexual violence in the Rome Statute. From 1997 onwards, various NGOs like the Women's Caucus for Gender Justice in the ICC started providing papers, exposing gaps that ensured many countries' support towards the inclusion of gender perspective by the time of Rome Conference in June 1998. In contrast to previous Statutes like ICTR and ICTY, Rome Statute includes rape and other sexual crimes as under Crimes against Humanity, war crimes, in violation of grave breaches of the Geneva Conventions and in violation of common Article 3.

VIOLENCE AGAINST WOMEN IN INDIA

As it is rightly said, 'violence against women'[21] is not a straightforward concept.[22] In India, the violence ranges from female foeticide, domestic abuse, dowry deaths, rapes, honour-killings, forced marriages, child marriages, female genital mutilation, harassment (in-person and/or online) and so on.[23] Since independence, the Indian government has passed several laws which aim at curbing violence against women. These laws are keeping in mind several societal evils that plague our society such as the caste system and patriarchy. However, according to several independent surveys and the numbers recorded by National Crime Records Bureau tell a different story.

National Crime Records Bureau released the report for the year 2017, in 2019.[24] It recorded that, 3,59,849 cases of crimes against women were recorded in the country, for the year 2017. The report also stated, that, "Majority of cases under crimes against women were registered under 'Cruelty by Husband or his Relatives' (27.9%) followed by 'Assault on Women with Intent to Outrage her Modesty' (21.7%), 'Kidnapping & Abduction of Women' (20.5%) and 'Rape' (7.0%)". These are only the reported cases on woman but there is no survey for transgender women.

There are several provisions in the Indian legal system that caters to curbing violence against woman in this day and age. The Indian Penal Code has several provisions, ranging from rape,[25] to outraging modesty of a woman[26] and even abetment of suicide of women.[27] Besides that, there are several Acts which directly affect women, such as The Dowry Prohibition Act, 1961, The Indecent Representation of Women (Prohibition) Act, 1986, The Commission of Sati Prevention Act, 1987 and also The Protection of women from Domestic Violence Act, 2005.

The problem of violence against women persists, so much so that, India has often been placed as #1 among the worst countries in the world for women.[28] This statement should be shocking, because we have stringent laws in place, we have several goddesses that Hindus in India pray too, we even call India or Bharat a 'mata' or mother. The Indian culture is big on glorifying some roles for women, but not protecting them. As we can see in this case decided by the High Court of Karnataka, in *Rakesh v. State of Karnataka*, the learned Judge allowed the accused his pre-arrest bail application because the alleged rape victim had 'slept' after the ordeal and that was a very unbecoming conduct for an Indian woman.[29] While these comments were later expunged,[30] they betrayed how deep-rooted our sense of patriarchy is.

In the case of *Raja v. State of Karnataka*,[31] the Supreme Court decided the case on the victim's conduct, stating that it was "not at all consistent with those of an unwilling, terrified and anguished victim of forcible intercourse". The same happened in the *Mahmood Farooqui v. GNCTD* case, where a women's 'no' was seen as a 'feeble yes', because she didn't protest strongly enough. The apex court also looked at if the alleged victim was habituated to sex and if she had marks on her body to decide whether it was rape or consensual sex in the two cases of *Pratap Mishra v. The State of Orissa*[32] and the famous *Mathura case*.[33] Even in that in famous case from a prominent law school, where three male law students blackmailed their female classmate into repeatedly raping her because they had some nude pictures of her. The Court noted on her promiscuous attitude[34] while granting bail to the three male law students.

CONCLUSION

It is strange that the police, the prosecutors, the court, the media and the society at large looks at the victim of rape's past to decide whether the incident happened. This is the logic that we apply for thieves, when a person accused of thievery has committed the crime before and accordingly a decision is made. If the same logic was applied in cases of murder, we will have to check if the victim of murder has been murdered before, but does that make sense? The same country which celebrates a festival where tying of a sacred thread is a symbol of protecting women. The same country which gives the name of 'ma' or 'mata' to idols, cows and the country itself, as a form of respect but it fails to protect, respect and believe its own women?

Prior to the pandemic, India was growing at an alarming rate, the economy was doing decently well, we had the support of several countries from the global north, we were (and sometimes still are) seen as the leaders of South Asia, if not whole of Asia. The pandemic has slowed things now, and there has been a realization, the rapid growth that India was making internationally was not being reflected internally. The illiteracy rates are still high, there is a stark difference between economic classes, the crime rates are still high, and some parts of the society still behaves that its part of the dark ages. The need of the hour is for the people of India to believe in its women: all *bharat mata bhakts* should start respecting and believing in *bharat mata's* daughters.

END NOTES

1. Dr. Vivian C. Fox, *Historical Perspectives on Violence Against Women*, 4 JIWS 15, 20 (2002)
2. *Id* at 17
3. *Id* at 19
4. SDG Knowledge Platforms, *Committee on the Elimination of Discrimination Against Women*, SDG KNOWLEDGE PLATFORMS (Jul. 14, 2020, 3:31 PM), https://sustainabledevelopment.un. org/ index.php?page=view&type=30022&nr=108&menu=3170
5. CEDAW, *General Recommendations*, OHCHR, (Jul. 14, 2020, 3:31 PM), https://www.ohchr.org/EN/HRBodies/CEDAW/Pages/ Recommendations.aspx
6. CEDAW, General Recommendation No. 12: Violence against Women, (Jul. 12, 2020, 11:22 PM), https://tbinternet.ohchr.org/ Treaties/CEDAW/Shared%20Documents/1_Global/ INT_CEDAW_GEC_5831_E.pdf
7. CEDAW, General Recommendation No. 14: Female Circumcision, (Jul. 12, 2020, 11:20 PM), https://tbinternet.ohchr.org/Treaties/ CEDAW/Shared%20Documents/1_Global/INT_CEDAW_ GEC_3729_E.pdf
8. United Nations Treaty Collection, *Convention on the Elimination of Discrimination Against Women*, (Jul. 14, 2020, 3:31 PM), https:/ /treaties.un.org/Pages/ViewDetails.aspx?src=TREATY& mtdsg_no=IV- 8&chapter=4&lang=en
9. UNGA, 48th Session, A/RES/48/104, (Jul. 13, 2020, 1:45 PM), https://www.un.org/ga/search/view_doc.asp?symbol=A/RES/48/104

10. UN Women, https://www.unwomen.org/en
11. UN, International Day for the Elimination of Violence against Women 25 November, (Jul. 11, 2020, 1:29 PM), https://www.un.org/en/events/endviolenceday/
12. UN Women, Commission on the Status of Women, (Jul. 12, 2020, 11:20 PM), https://www.unwomen.org/en/csw
13. UNDP, 5 Gender Equality, (Jul. 12, 2020, 11:45 PM), https://www.undp.org/content/undp/en/home/sustainable-development-goals/goal-5-gender-equality.html
14. UN, International Day for the Elimination of Violence against Women 25 November, (Jul. 11, 2020, 1:29 PM), https://www.un.org/en/events/endviolenceday/
15. UN Women, Facts and figures: Ending violence against women, (Jul. 19, 2020, 7:12 PM), https://www.unwomen.org/en/what-we-do/ending-violence-against-women/facts-and-figures
16. UN Women, Facts and figures: Ending violence against women, (Jul. 19, 2020, 7:12 PM), https://www.unwomen.org/en/what-we-do/ending-violence-against-women/facts-and-figures
17. Niamh Hayes, Sisyphus Wept: *Prosecuting Sexual Violence at the International Criminal Court, The Ashgate Research Companion to International Criminal Law Critical Perspectives* (2013)
18. ICTR, Chamber I, Prosecutor v. Jean-Paul Akayesu, Judgement, 2 September 1998, ICTR-96-4-T
19. United Nations General Assembly, Vienna Declaration and Platform of Action, A/CONF.157/24, 12 July 1993; Fourth World Conference on Women, 17 October 1995, A/CONF.177/20
20. United Nations Office Of The High Commissioner for Human Rights, The Elimination of Violence against Women, res. 1997/44
21. Charlotte Watts & Cathy Zimmerman, *Violence against Women: Global Scope and Magnitude*, 359 THE LANCET, 1232 (2002).
22. A. Dutt, *Locating Patriarchy In Violence Against Women In India: Social, Legal And Alternative Responses*, 4 IJOSS 212, 213 (2018)
23. United Nations Human Rights Office of the High Commissioner, *Women's Rights are Human Rights*, (Jul. 11, 2020, 1:29 PM),https://www.ohchr.org/Documents/Events/WHRD/WomenRightsAreHR.pdf
24. Special Correspondent, *Uttar Pradesh tops in crimes against women, says NCRB report*, THE HINDU, https://www.thehindu.com/news/national/other-states/uttar-pradesh-tops-in-crimes-against-

women-says-ncrb- report/article29760974.ece

25. Section 376, IPC
26. Section 354C, IPC
27. Section 306, IPC
28. Thompson Reuters Foundation, *The world's most dangerous countries for women 2018*, https://poll2018.trust.org/;Frank Jacobs, *U.S. in top 10 most dangerous countries for women*, BIG THINK, https://bigthink.com/strange- maps/worst-countries-for-women?rebelltitem=1#rebelltitem1
29. *Rakesh v. State of Karnataka*, Order, Criminal Petition No. 2427 of 2020, https://www.livelaw.in/news- updates/not-the-way-our-women-react-when-they-are-ravished-karnataka-hc-on-rape-victim-claiming-to-have- slept-after-offence-read-order-158855
30. *Rakesh v. State of Karnataka*, Order, Criminal Petition No. 2427 of 2020, https://www.livelaw.in/top- stories/karnataka-hc-expunges-controversial-remarks-about-womans-conduct-from-bail-order-in-rape-case- 159341
31. *Raja & Ors vs State Of Karnataka*, (Reportable), https://indiankanoon.org/doc/134419727/.
32. *Pratap Misra And Ors. vs State Of Orissa*, (1977) AIR 1307 (India)
33. *Tuka Ram And Anr vs State Of Maharashtra*, (1979) AIR 185 (India)
34. *Vikas Garg & Others v. State of Haryana*, Criminal Main 23962 & 26930 Of 2017 In CRegular First Appeal No. S-2396-Sb Of 2017 & Cr. M. No. 26910-11 Of 2017 In Regular First Appeal No. D-653 & 662 Of 2017, https://www.legitquest.com/case/vikas-garg-others-v-state-of-haryana/FB088

11

An Analytical Study on Women as a Victim of Violence in India

Monjushna Goswami

The traditional Indian society places women in a very high regards, the Vedas glorified women as the mother, the creator, and one who gives life and worshipped her as a Devi or Goddess. However, in modern times women are viewed and portrayed as sex objects, she is treated inferior to men in various societal spheres and functions, this has created a huge gender bias between the men and women where even the men think that their wrongdoings towards women cannot be penalised. Crime against women refers to the physical, mental or sexual violence committed against women, typically by a man. The attempt is based on secondary data collected from various articles related to woman and crime along with the National Crime Records Bureau statistics of India and also Indian Penal Code, 1860 (Bare Act).

UNDERSTANDING WOMEN AND CRIME: THE TRUTH

To study women and crime is all about direct or indirect physical or mental cruelity to women. Crime against women which include abuse any sort of physical aggression or misbehave. When crime is committed at home it becomes domestic crime which involves family members such as children, spouse, parents or servants. Domestic crime may involve different means such as hitting, kicking, biting, throwing objects etc. It also includes threats, sexual abuse, and emotional abuse, controlling or domineering. According to National Crime Records Bureau, domestic violence against women figures as the top category of violence against women in 2018. As per the data, a total of 89,097 cases related to crimes against women were registered across India in 2018. The figures indicate not much has improved when compared to the figure of 86,001 cases registered under this head in 2017. The crime rate per lakh women population is 58.8 in 2018 in comparison to 57.9 in 2017. Out of the total crimes registered under the Indian Penal Code against the women, the majority of the cases were registered under the 'cruelty by husband or his relatives' at 31.9 per cent. This was followed by 'assault on women with intent to outrage her modesty' at 27.6 per cent. The cases of the 'kidnapping and abduction of women stood at 22.5 per cent and the rape cases comprised 10.3 per cent of the overall crime figures.

A total of 50,74,634 cognizable crimes, comprising 31,32,954 IPC and 19,41,680 Special and Local Laws (SLL) crimes, were registered in 2018. Reviewing Indian Penal Codes and statistics of National Crime Records Bureau provides the real picture relating to crime against women.

RAPE

India is considered to be the world's most dangerous country for sexual violence against women. Rape is one of the most common crimes in India which have increase tremendously. The offence can be categorized in various aspects as a rape of a minor girl, rape of a woman (Sec 376), rape with murder (Sec 376C), gang rape (Sec 376D), etc. Section 376 provides punishment for committing the heinous crime of rape. Section 376(1) provides a minimum sentence of seven years of imprisonment that may extend to life imprisonment and fine. Section 376(2) provides punishment not less than ten years of imprisonment but may extend to imprisonment for life or death or fine. 376 D lays down the punishment for gang rape. Where a woman is raped by more than one person with a common intention, each of them shall be liable for the offence and shall be punished with rigorous imprisonment for not less than twenty years which may extend to lifetime imprisonment and fine.

KIDNAPPING

The term kidnapping refer to either kidnapping from India or kidnapping from lawful guardianship. Section 360 of the IPC states that whoever convey any person beyond India without his /her consent is said to kidnap that person from India whoever takes a minor away without his /her or guardian consent means to kidnap that person from his/her lawful guardian (Sec 361). In 2017, a total of 96,650 kidnapped or abducted persons (24,721 male and 71,929 female) were recovered, of which 94,658 persons were recovered alive and 1,992 persons were dead. The rate of kidnapping and abduction was the highest in Delhi with 27.6 cases per one lakh of population followed by Assam with 23.9 cases and Haryana with 15.7 cases. The punishment for this purpose is upto 7 years and fine. Sec 366 of IPC defines kidnapping, abducting or including woman to compel her marriage and forceful sexual relations for which the offender can be punished with imprisonment upto 10 years and fine.

DOMESTIC VIOLENCE

Domestic violence which is also called intimate partner violence occurs between people in an intimate relationship. Abusive relationships always involve an imbalance of power and control. Domestic violence against women figures as the top category of violence against women in 2018. As per the data, a total of 89,097 cases related to crimes against women were registered across India in 2018. The two crimes against women that relate directly to domestic violence in India are 'dowry death' and 'cruelty by husband and relatives'. The Protection of Women from Domestic Violence Act, 2015 was passed in 2005. In the 10 years since the Act was passed, over 1,000,000 cases have been filed across the country.

EVE TEASING

Many countries have taken action in recent times to address harassment in the work place and violence in the home, but little attention has been paid to sexual harassment in public places, specifically during women's journey to work and school. In developing countries, many more women are seeking education and employment than previously, which has increased the opportunity for sexual harassment in public places. In India, the study location, this harassment is known as 'eve teasing'. Such act which insults the modesty of woman which may not necessarily involve any physical force is brought under the shade of this provision through Section 509. Any person who commits an offence under Section 509 shall be punished with simple imprisonment for a term which may extend to three years with fine.

SEXUAL HARASSMENT

707 incidents of sexual harassment were reported in 2018 in shelter homes in India. The maximum number of shelter homes have been reported from Uttar Pradesh (288), followed by Maharashtra (161), Andhra Pradesh (62), MP (61) and Haryana (49). There were 730 reports of incidents of sexual harassment of women in the public transport system and 401 reports of such incidents at the workplace in 2018, up from 599 and 479 in 2017. Section 354A of IPC if any person commit an act of sexual harassment such as physical contact or asking for sexual favour or pornography, he shall be rigorously imprisoned upto 3 years and fine. While if any person commit an act of sexual harassment of the by sexually coloured remark, he shall be rigorously imprisoned upto 1years and fine.

ACID ATTACK

India tops the charts when it comes to acid attacks. Though the sale of acids without proper information has been banned by government of India, but still acid attacks are in trend to threaten and hurt women. There are so many cases of acid attack that happen but never get filed especially in our hinterlands because in so many of these cases settlement happens outside the judiciary. Several other external factors like caste, class, power also come into play when registering such cases as asserted by Ashish Shukla of Chaanv Foundation. The percentage of cases of acid attacks that the courts disposed, of all the cases that went for trial, was 6.6 percent (27 cases out of 407) in the year 2016. It is only in 2017 that the percentage went up to 9.9 percent (44 cases out of 442). But, in 2018, it again came down to 6.11 percent cases (32 cases out of 523) reflecting that the system is unable to provide swift justice in the matter. In all, 228 acid attacks were reported in the country in 2018. In 2016, the number stood at 223 and rose to 244 in 2017. The Criminal Law (Amendment) Act, 2013 under Section 326A and 326B intend to make specific provision for punishment in the case of acid attack. Section 326A focuses on voluntarily causing grievous hurt by using acid. Under this section, whosoever causes permanent or partial damage or burns, disfigures or disables any part of the body of a person or causes grievous hurt by throwing acid with an intention to cause such injury or hurt will be punished with imprisonment of at least ten years which may extend to life imprisonment with fine. Section 326B has more legislative focus on the act of throwing or attempting to throw acid with the intention of causing grievous hurt. The punishment under this section is imprisonment of not less than five years with fine which may extend upto seven years.

DOWRY DEATH

Dowry death are more common in rural areas of India where young women are murdered or driven to suicide by continuous harassment and torture by husbands and in-laws in an effort to extort an increased dowry. The number of such deaths has increased in the recent years. In India according to 2016 statistic there were over 2,470 dowry death cases reported in UP followed by Bihar with 987 cases, MP 629, West Bengal 535, Rajasthan 462, Orissa 397, Jharkhand 278, Haryana 260, Maharashtra 248, Karnataka 234, Andhra Pradesh 193, Delhi 162 and Assam 157 cases. The Dowry Prohibition Act of 1961 prohibits the request, payment or acceptance of a dowry, 'as consideration for the marriage', where 'dowry' is defined as a gift demanded or given as a precondition for a marriage.

WOMEN TRAFFICKING (Section 370, 370A, 372, 373)

The trafficking of women for sexual exploitation is an international, organized, criminal phenomenon that has grave consequences for the safety, welfare and human rights of its victims. It violates basic human rights, and totally destroying victims' lives. Thai and hill tribe women and girls are trafficked to Japan, Malaysia, South Africa, Bahrain, Australia, Singapore, Europe, Canada and the United States for sexual and labor exploitation. In the Mewat district of Haryana (India) women are sold as sex slaves to men and then sold again in a 'bizarre form of currency'. For many years now, girls are trafficked from the poor regions of Assam, Bihar, Jharkhand, Odisha, eastern Uttar Pradesh and West Bengal with promises of employment or marriage and are sold in this district. According to the NCRB the highest incidence of children and women being trafficked were observed from the cities of Mumbai and Kolkata. In 2015, only 4,203 trafficking cases were investigated in India. In 2014, 76% of people trafficked in India were women and girls. West Bengal was second both in number of missing children and women from 2016-18.

Mumbai and Pune appear to be the most vulnerable. Mumbai recorded the highest number of missing women during 2017 and 2018 with 4,718 and 5,201 women missing respectively. The Pune was second with 2,576 cases in 2017 and 2,504 in 2018 according to NCRB.

In West Bengal, Kolkata reported the increase in number of missing women cases to 2,584 cases in 2018 from 357 cases in 2017. In Madhya Pradesh, Indore retained the top position in 2017 and 2018 with 1,755 and 2,458 cases of missing women respectively. Section 370 describes trafficking which includes minor girls, trafficking for the purpose of exploitation etc. Section 372 and 373 states the buying and selling of minor for the purpose of prostitution. The imprisonment term varies in each offence and ranges from 3 years to life imprisonment and also fine.

CYBER CRIMES

Though crime against women is on a rise in all fields being a victim of cybercrime could be most traumatic experience for a woman. Especially in India where the society looks down upon the women, and the law doesn't even properly recognize cybercrimes. According to the NCRB, 21,796 instances of cyber crime were recorded in 2017, 4,242 about 19.5% were committed against women, and 88 against children. The cyber crimes against women were related to cyber blackmail or threats, cyber pornography or hosting or publishing obscene sexual materials, cyber stalking or cyber bullying of women, defamation, or morphing and indecent representation of women, etc. Cybercrime is a term for any illegal activity that uses a computer as its primary means of commission Women especially young girls inexperienced in cyber world, who have been newly introduced to the internet and fail to understand the vices of internet, and fall into the bait of cyber criminals & bullies. There are several cyber crimes such as bullying, abushing, pornography etc. which are happening each day against women. These crimes have several punishments under the Information Technology Act, 2000 which range from imprisonment upto 3 years and fine.

OUTRAGING THE MODESTY OF WOMEN (SECTION 354)

Section 354, IPC deals with the offence of molestation i.e. assault to woman with intent to outrage her modesty. It aims to protect women against any sort of indecent behaviour by others which is derogatory to her modesty. This offence is not just against the individual but also against the society and public morality. Therefore, if any person uses criminal force upon a woman with an intention to outrage the modesty of a woman, he is deemed to be punished with an imprisonment of not less than one year which may extend upto five years with fine. Incidents of assault on women with intent to outrage her modesty in the country have increased by 0.2 percent (from 82,235 cases in 2014 to 82,422 cases in 2015) during 2015 over the previous year. Maharashtra (11,713 cases) has reported the highest number of such crimes followed by Madhya Pradesh (8,049 cases) and Uttar Pradesh (7,885 cases). Delhi UT has reported the highest crime rate of assault on women with intent to outrage her modesty cases (57.8) compared to the national average of 13.6. A total of 82,800 victims were reported under 82,422 cases of assault on woman with intent to outrage her modesty cases in the country during the year 2015. Under IPC section 354 and 354B whoever assaults or uses criminal force intending to outrage her modesty will have 1yr-5yrs imprisonment or disrobing her or compelling her to be naked will have 3yr-7yrs imprisonment.

HONOUR KILLING

An honor killing or shame killing is the murder of a member of a family, due to the perpetrators belief that the victim has brought shame or dishonor upon the family, or has violated the principles of a community or a religion with an honor culture. Typical reasons include divorcing or separating from their spouse, refusing to enter an arranged, child or forced marriage, being in a relationship or having associations with social groups outside the family that is strongly disapproved by one's family, having premarital or extramarital sex, becoming the victim of rape or sexual assault, dressing style, jewelry and accessories which are deemed inappropriate, engaging in non heterosexual relations or renouncing a faith. National Crime Records Bureau recorded a total of 28 cases in 2014, 251 cases in 2015 and 77 cases in 2016 and only one instance of honor killing in 2018 in the country. It violates certain fundamental rights in the constitution of India, including the right to life, and liberty which includes the right to bodily integrity, and the right to choose whom to associate with. A statistical analysis in different pictorial form is brought forth on the various crimes committed against women.

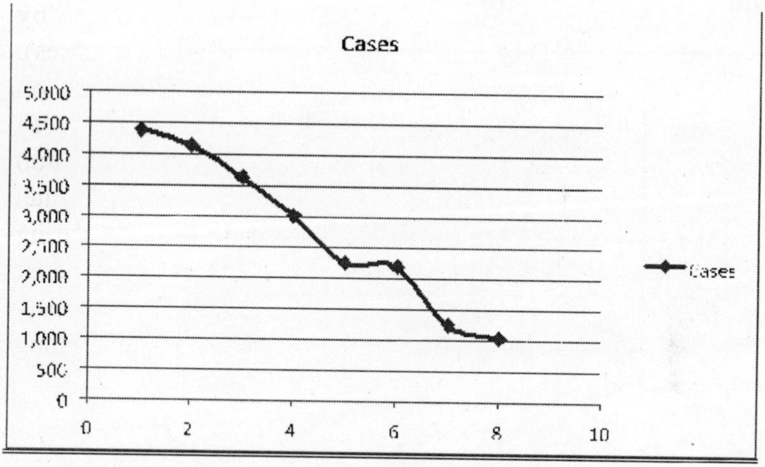

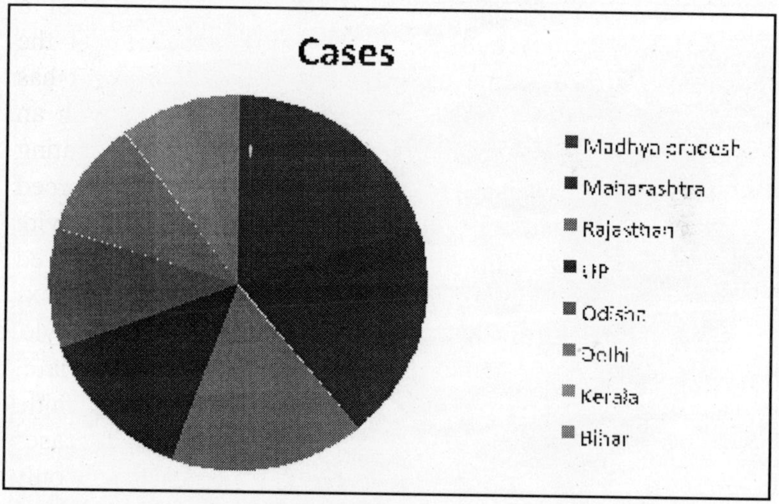

Diagram represents the states with highest number of rape cases in India. Data collected by the NCRB.

The above diagram represents the states with highest number of rape cases in India. Data collected by the NCRB.

State-wise data of highest number of kidnapping cases in India

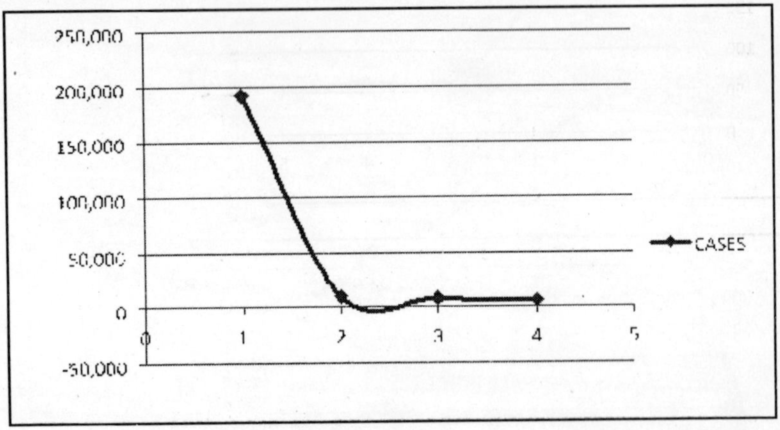

State-wise data of highest number of kidnapping cases in India

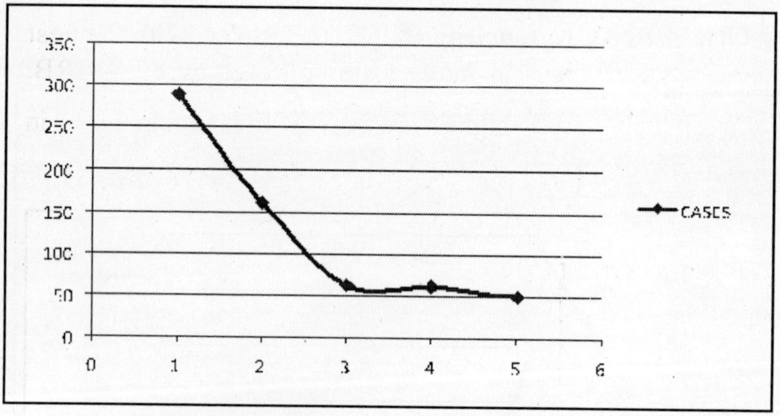

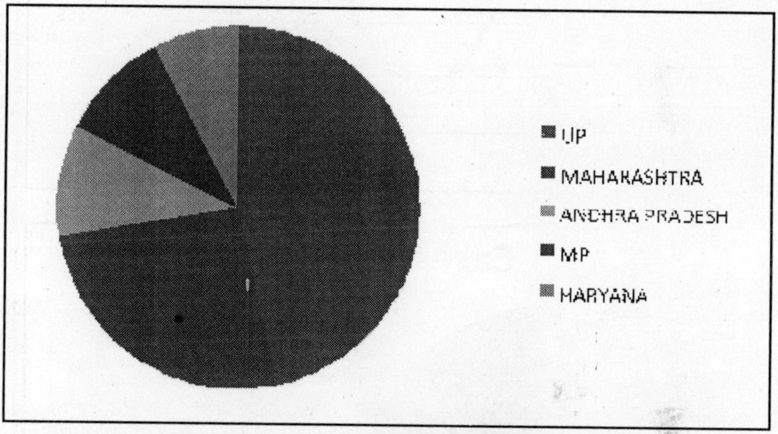

Diagrams show cases from different shelter homes of different states in India pertaining to woman and sexual harassment collected by National Crime Records Bureau in 2018.

The above diagrams shows cases from different shelter homes of different states in India pertaining to woman and sexual harassment collected by National Crime Records Bureau in 2018.

ACID ATTACK CASES IN 2016, 2017 & 2018.

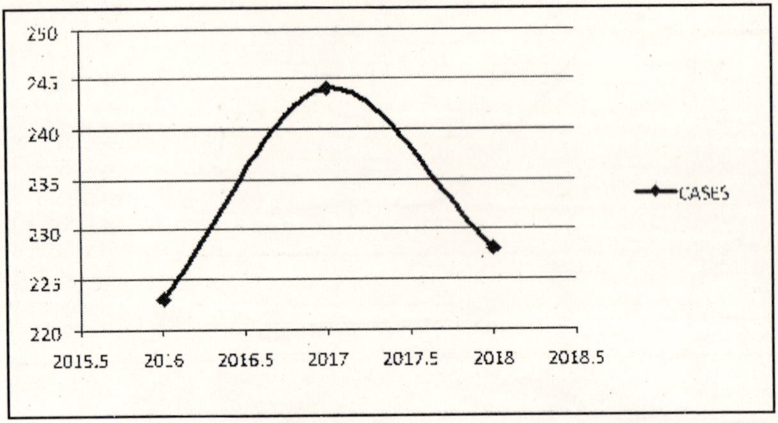

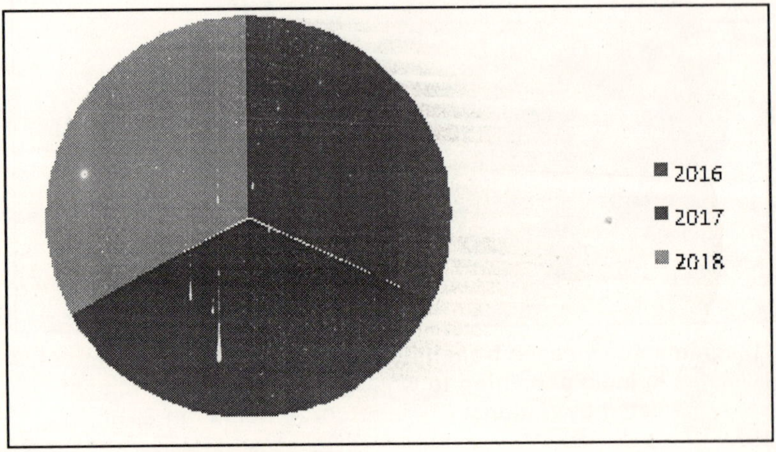

Acid Attack cases in 2016, 2017 & 2018.

DOWRY DEATH CASES REPORTED IN DIFFERENT STATE OF INDIA DURING 2016.

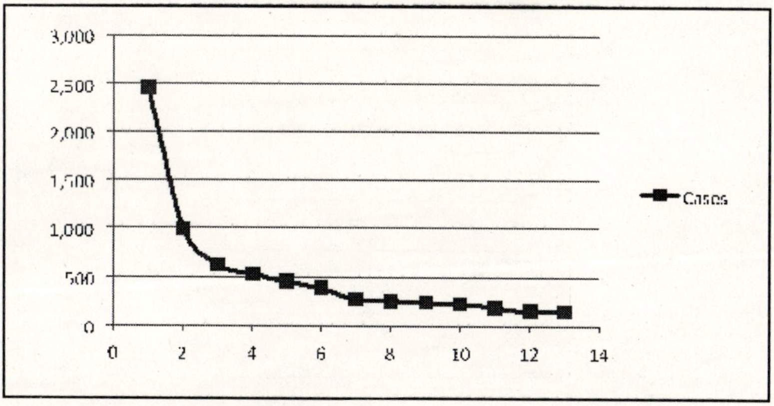

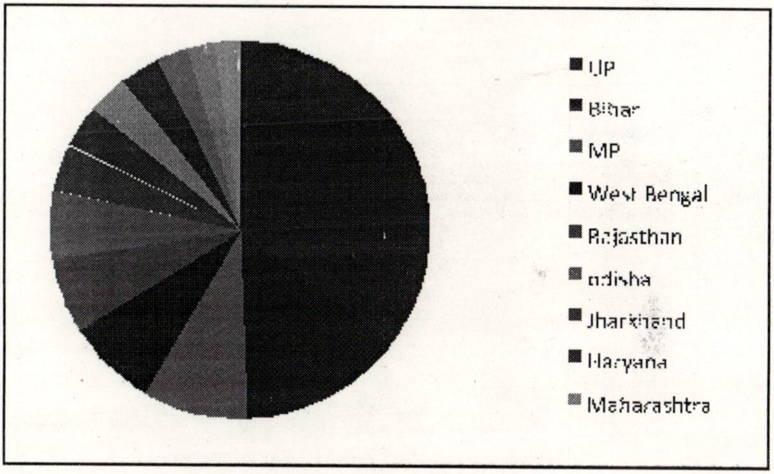

Dowry death cases reported in different state of India during 2016.

WOMEN TRAFFICKING CASES IN 2017 & 2018

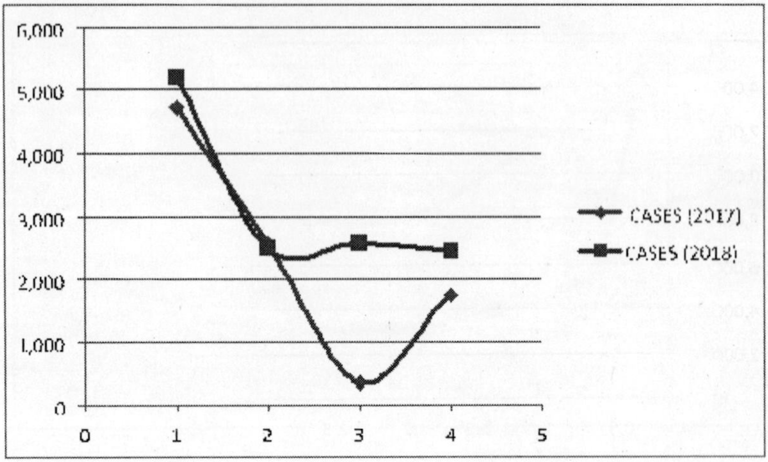

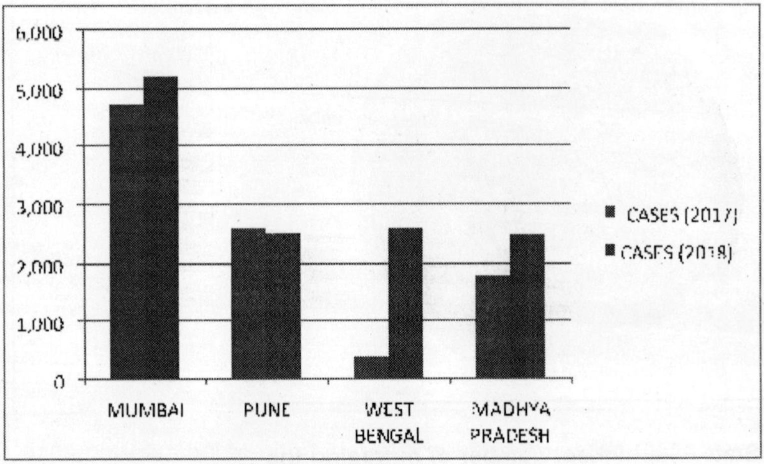

Women trafficking cases in 2017 & 2018 (NCRB report)

STATE WITH HIGHEST NUMBER OF OUTRAGING THE MODESTY OF WOMEN CASES IN INDIA

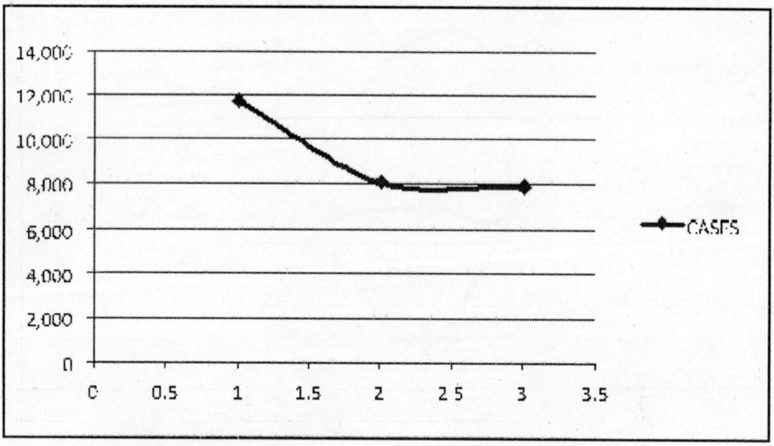

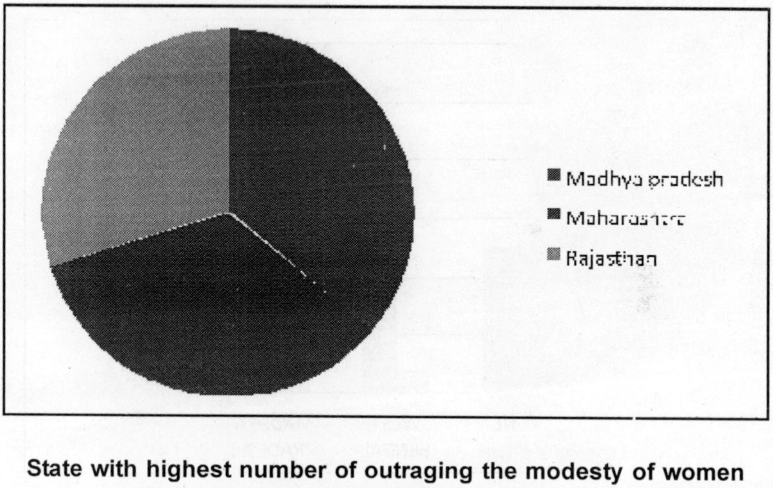

State with highest number of outraging the modesty of women cases in India (NCRB report)

HONOR KILLING CASES IN 2016, 2017 & 2018

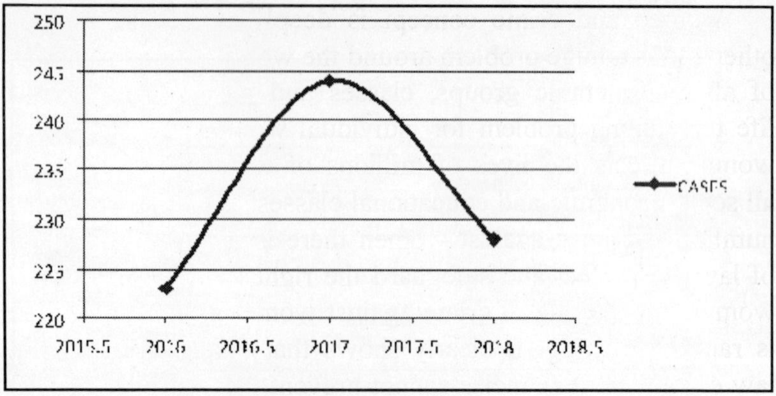

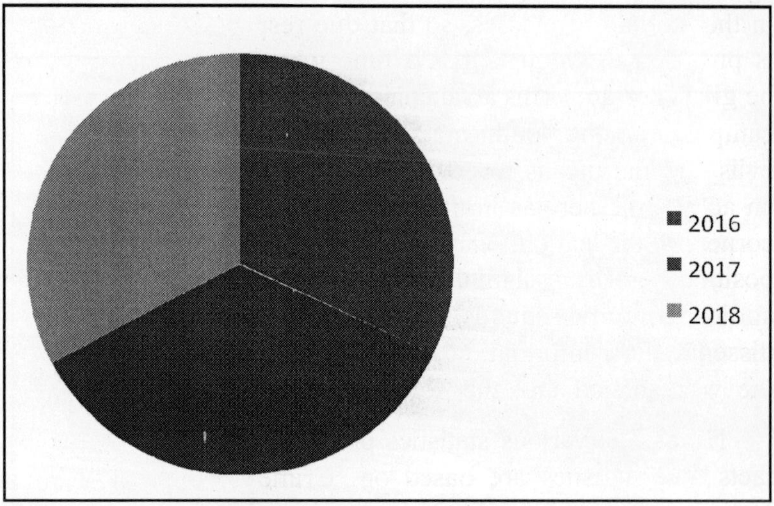

Honor Killing cases in 2016, 2017 & 2018

CONCLUSION AND SUGGESTION

Women and crime concept is deeply connected to each other and is a huge problem around the world. It affects women of all races, ethnic groups, classes and nationalities. It is a life threatening problem for individual women. Crime against women affects the lives of millions of women worldwide in all socio-economic and educational classes. With the increasing number of crimes against women there is increase in number of laws to protect and safeguard the rights and interest of the women but the rate of crime against women and victimization is rapidly growing. It clearly shows that only legislation and law enforcement agencies cannot prevent the incident of crime against women. There is need of social awakening and change in the attitude of masses, so that due respect and equal status is provided to women. It is a time when the women need to be given her due. This awakening can be brought by education, campaign among youth, making them aware of existing social evils and the means to eradicate same. Mass media can play an active role here as in the present days it has reached every corner of the nation. Various NGOs can hold a responsible position here by assigning them with the task of highlighting socio-economic causes leading to such crimes and by disseminating information about their catastrophic effect on the womanhood and the society at large.

Note: The various statistics provided here is based on the facts and statistics are based on 'Crime in India' report of National Crime Records Bureau.

SELECTED READINGS

1. Amay Bajaj (Crimes Against Women - A Legal Perspective)
2. The Indian Penal Code, 1860 (Bare Act)
3. Government of India (2000). 'Crime in India'. New Delhi: National Crime Records Bureau.

4. NCRB (National Crime Record Bureau). (2016). *'Crime in India'* report
5. Borah, P. (2008). 'Examining Media Content: A Case Study of Newspaper Coverage of Dowry in India, 1996-2006'. *Asian Journal of Communication*, 18(4), 379-395
6. Reported dowry death cases in India - by state and union territory 2016 , Published by Sandhya Keelery, Sep 23, 2019
7. Kalra, G., & Bhugra, D. (2013) 'Sexual violence against women: Understanding Cross cultural Intersections'. *Indian Journal of Psychiatry*, 55(3), 244

12

Women and Crime: Selected Cases

Cases Brought to Justice Due to Social Pressure Bringing to the Fore Shoddy Investigations, Cover-ups, and use of Circumstantial Evidence

Vaibhav Kumar Garg

PRELUDE

Social pressure is a potent tool to bring cases to justice. The judiciary on multiple occasions has hastened the justice delivery process owing to public pressure. So significant is the power of social pressure that public campaigning for justice has gradually become a trend in the Indian judicial process. The trend is best demonstrated by the outrage that followed the 2012 Delhi gang-rape case. However, the birth of this movement of public activism can be traced to the famous cases of Priyadarshani Mattoo and Jessica Lal.

The murders of Priyadarshani Mattoo and Jessica Lal shocked public conscience. The two women embodied the better aspects of modern India. Priyadarshani as a student at Delhi's premier law college was the ideal girl any parent would want. Jessica, on the other hand, symbolized the aspirations of the Indian youth as a successful model enjoying her life in the nation's capital. Their murders struck a chord with the public because of how relatable they were as normal and respectable women. Public authorities in both the cases failed to do their duty in seeing to it that the law was followed. Priyadarshani's killer was acquitted by the trial judge even though it was clear that he had committed the crime. In Jessica's case, the police watched on as the murderer bribed and intimidated his way to freedom.

Where the public authorities failed, the media succeeded. The media and the public played an instrumental role in bringing the murderers of the two women to justice. Demonstrations were held in Delhi demanding that justice is brought to the women. The media covered the trials in minute detail, thereby forcing the judiciary to take prompt notice of the cases. This can be seen from the fact that both the cases were heard on a day to day basis by the Delhi High Court.

The social pressure in both the cases was effective. The killers of Priyadarshani Mattoo and Jessica Lal are now serving life imprisonment terms for their acts. Even more important is that these two cases showed that the judiciary is open to the public's opinions and not as deaf as most suspect. As soon as the public expressed its displeasure with the court proceedings, the judges took prompt action to satisfy public demands for justice. Trial Court judgments of acquittal were overruled, investigating agencies criticized and the guilty convicted. And all of that was done quickly and efficiently. The two cases mark a new epoch in the Indian legal system.

Now, the victims of crime know that they are not at the mercy of a judge's discretion. The media can lobby to make the judiciary take action. A victim now has the awareness that they can advocate their case even outside of court, which would allow them to get a fair hearing inside it.

However, the fact that the judiciary has to rely on outside support to uphold the law is disheartening. Ideally, the judicial process should be independent and fair. This is so because the judiciary has the responsibility to protect the rights of the public. The judiciary should not be prone to manipulation by rich individuals as that undermines the credibility of the entire process of justice delivery. But the fact that the judiciary is prone to such manipulation shows that it still needs some time to mature. The lower judiciary of India still suffers from indifference and sometimes incompetence. A lot of poor litigants do not get a proper hearing because they cannot afford good lawyers to represent them in court. The rich on the other hand have the ability to get away with blatant crimes by employing top lawyers and also taking the help of bribes and intimidation. Here, attempt is made to analyze the role of social pressure plays in bringing cases to justice. To highlight the role of the public and the media, the cases of Priyadarshani Mattoo and Jessica Lal are analyzed as these two cases present the most potent examples of the power of social pressure.

PRIYADARSHANI MATTOO'S CASE

Introduction

Serious questions are raised when a judge states a man guilty, yet declines to convict him. After all, why would a judge refuse to punish a man he proclaims to be guilty? As baffling as it might sound this is exactly what the trial court judge in Priyadarshani Mattoo's case did. In a judgment which shocked the nation, the judge apologetically mentioned about the accused that "I know that he is the man who committed the crime. (But) I acquit him, giving him the benefit of doubt."[1]

You would think that given the wide powers conferred on a judge, he would have the authority to decide a case as he feels to be just. Sadly though, even the long hands of justice are tied when the very investigating agencies which are meant to uphold the rule of law aim to deceive the judiciary. The trial court judge glaringly brought the judiciary's limitations to public scrutiny when he failed to punish the guilty man. Now, why was this guilty man acquitted? The answer lies in a perusal of Priyadarshani Mattoo's murder and the trial that followed.

Priyadarshani was murdered by a man who loved her. This man, Santosh Singh, was Priyadarshani's senior at Delhi University's prestigious Faculty of Law. Santosh killed her after she rejected his romantic advances toward her. After the act was done, Santosh and his father actively tried to alter the course of the case to escape punishment.

Priyadarshani Mattoo's case ideally fits into the narrative of a rich and powerful father subverting the law to protect his son. Santosh Singh was the son of an influential Delhi police officer appointed as the Commissioner of Police in Delhi. Acting under the influence of Santosh's father, officials of the Delhi Police tried to conceal evidence in the case so that Santosh could be acquitted of his charges. For instance, the Delhi Police failed to produce a key witness who had seen Santosh enter the house in which Priyadarshani was residing on the day of her death. This witness, the servant of the house, was later easily found by a reporter in his village in Bihar, thus showing the negligence of the Delhi Police.[2]

However, the unethical conduct of the Delhi Police was circumvented by social pressure which altered the course of the judgment. Media rose to the occasion and picked up on the fact that despite many clinching shreds of evidence, Singh managed to walk out of jail, as a free man, without being proven guilty of a single charge.

Intense media coverage by various news channels and newspapers was creating strong pressure on the CBI as it submitted a fresh appeal against the verdict of the District Court in the Delhi High Court. Due to the severe and increasing media scrutiny, the hearing of the case was taken up on a daily basis and finally, the Delhi High Court pronounced Santosh Singh guilty.[3]

Brief Facts

Santosh had feelings for Priyadarshani, Santosh used to follow Priyadarshani in a manner akin to stalking even after graduating from the University. On numerous occasions, Santosh harassed and intimidated her. Increasingly frustrated by Santosh's behaviour, she filed a complaint against him with the police as a last recourse. The police summoned Santosh to the police station and curtly told him to behave himself. Further, Priyadarshani was given a Personal Security Officer for her protection.[4]

Santosh felt aggrieved by the complaint. He retaliated by alleging to the University that Priyadarshani was studying two courses at the same time and thus was violating the University's rules. However, on a perusal of the facts, the University found the allegations to be baseless. But Santosh had still further plans of revenge as was tragically found on the day of Priyadarshani's death.

Priyadarshani was found brutally murdered at a relative's house. Suresh was the main suspect from the start since Priyadarshani's relatives knew of his previous conduct and therefore suspected him of being behind Priyadarshani's death. Following Suresh's denial of any wrong-doing on his part, the case went to trial.[5]

Trial

The Additional Session Judge, G.P Tharejaheavily criticized the role of the Delhi Police in the trial. "There has been particular inaction by Delhi Police", he said, while observing that Santosh's father was probably involved in the subversion of the investigation process.[6]

Thareja acquitted Santosh Singh on the charge of rape and gave him the benefit of the doubt for murder. The judge held that due to the CBI failing to produce relevant circumstantial evidence in the case, the benefit of doubt ought to go in favour of Santosh Singh. The failure of the CBI mainly was with regard to their inability to produce Virender Prasad who was the servant in the house where Priyadarshani was found dead. Further, the trial court rejected the DNA evidence presented before it contending that it had tampered. Judge Thareja said that the CBI's failure to produce evidence had created a hole in the case which stopped it from being proved beyond a reasonable doubt.

Appeal

On October 17, 2006, Santosh Singh, who meanwhile had married and become a practicing lawyer in Delhi itself, was found guilty under Indian Penal Code sections 302 (murder) and 376 (rape). The verdict blames G.P Thareja's original judgment, "The trial judge acquitted the accused amazingly taking a perverse approach. It murdered justice and shocked the judicial conscience".[7] In particular, the verdict held that there were no lacunae in the DNA testing and that the combination of the forensic and circumstantial evidence was clinching. However, the bench agreed with the trial court's observation that police were reluctant to act on repeated complaints of harassment and stalking against Singh as his father was a senior IPS officer.[8] The verdict says "junior staff do not react to complaints against the relatives of their fraternity" and referred to the trial court's observation that the approach and working of the subordinate staff of Delhi Police clearly reflected that the rule of law "is not meant for those who enforce the law nor for their near relatives".

The verdict was reached on the basis of strong circumstantial evidence. Priyadarshini's father expressed satisfaction that justice had been achieved ten years after the gruesome murder.

In October 2010, the Supreme Court upheld the conviction of Santosh Kumar Singh but reduced the death sentence to life imprisonment.[9]

Status of Victims/Convicts

During the course of the trial, Suresh Singh got married and became a practicing lawyer at the Delhi High Court. Following, the Supreme Court's decision on his appeal, he has been serving his sentence of life imprisonment and on 21st May 2019 on the order of the Hon'ble High Court of Delhi, he was released on bail for the period of 3 weeks to write his law exams.[10]

JESSICA LAL'S CASE

Introduction

Jessica Lal's case is one of the most famous instances of social pressure leading to justice for the victim. Jessica Lal was a model residing in New Delhi. At a party held near the Qutub Minar, she was shot dead by Sidharth Vashisht, alias Manu Sharma. Manu Sharma was the son of the Excise Minister in the state of Haryana, "Venod Sharma." The trial judge at first acquitted Manu Sharma of the charges levelled against him but following protests from the public, the Delhi High Court found him to be guilty.[11]

The dispute between Jessica and Manu was trivial. Jessica Lal was serving as a celebrity bartender at the party. Manu Sharma, in an inebriated state, went to Jessica and asked her for a drink when the club was going to close. Jessica told Manu that she could not give him a drink to which Manu got angry and took out his gun. He first fired a shot at the ceiling. Immediately after that, he aimed his pistol at Jessica's temple and fired a shot. Jessica died on the spot. Realizing the implications of his act, Manu along with three other associates fled Delhi to Himachal Pradesh the moment after the murder. However, he was caught a few weeks later by the Delhi police.

Most people present at the party refused to give testimony to the events of the night. When Manu shot Jessica, most party-goers were present at the venue. However, Manu Sharma and his father bullied the possible witnesses into silence by exerting their political influence. As a result, the trial court acquitted Manu Sharma of the charges raised against him because of insufficient evidence.[12]

Following Manu Sharma's acquittal, there were large public protests demanding justice for Jessica. In Delhi, protests were held near India Gate demanding Manu Sharma be convicted. Numerous media houses also played their part in the protest including NDTV which launched a signature campaign to ask the President of India to intervene in the matter.[13]

Following the protests, the case was appealed to the Delhi High Court. Instead of the lax pace in which proceedings are normally conducted in the High Court, this case was tried on a day-to-day basis. Following the perusal of the evidence the High Court held Manu Sharma guilty for murder. On an appeal to the Supreme Court, the punishment was upheld and currently, he is serving a sentence of life imprisonment in the Tihar Jail.[14]

Trial

Manu Sharma was charged with murder and destruction of evidence among other offenses. Sharma's associates were charged with lesser offences which included conspiracy and harbouring a suspect.

The trial of the case was conducted at a snail's pace allowing most witnesses the time to withdraw their statements. In 2006, seven years after Jessica's death, the trial court finally gave a decision. The court acquitted Manu Sharma and his associates of all charges levelled against them citing a lack of evidence. As many as 32 witnesses had turned hostile against the prosecution during the course of the trial. The most prominent among them was actor Shyan Munshi who was near Jessica when she was shot. He had made a statement in Hindi to the police immediately after Jessica's shooting. Later he claimed that he did not know Hindi at all and therefore the testimony was false. However, his claim was later easily countered when a news agency conducted a sting in which they asked him to speak in Hindi to check his eligibility for a movie role, he spoke in fluent Hindi.[15]

The trial mentioned that the accused were acquitted because of the Delhi Police's failure to produce sufficient evidence. The Delhi Police failed to produce the weapon which had been used to fire at Jessica which was crucial to the prosecution's case. The Delhi Police had also failed to prove that the shot fired towards the roof and the one fired at Jessica belonged to the same cartridge.

Appeal

The High Court ruled that Sharma was guilty based on existing evidence, and also criticized the trial judge, S. L. Bhayana. The High Court criticized Bhayana for not giving enough importance to the testimonies of Bina Ramani and

Deepak Bhojwani. The High Court opined that there was non-application of mind on Bhayana's part and he gave the judgment with an intention to acquit Manu Sharma and his associates.[16]

Even more severe criticism was in store for Shayan Munshi, the principal witness for the prosecution. Regarding Munshi's testimony that two guns were involved, the judgment says: "In court, he has taken a somersault and came out with a version that there were two gentlemen at the bar counter. ... We have no manner of doubt that on this aspect he is telling a complete lie."

Ultimately, Manu Sharma was punished with a sentence of life imprisonment and a fine. The other accused were fined and given four years' rigorous imprisonment. A plea for Sharma to be sentenced to death was rejected on the grounds that the murder, although intentional, was not premeditated and Sharma was not considered to be a threat to society.

Sharma's lawyer announced that the decision would be appealed in Supreme Court because the judgment was wrong in holding Bina Ramani to be a witness. On 19 April 2010, the Supreme Court of India approved the sentences and said that the evidence regarding the actual incident, the testimonies of witnesses, the evidence connecting the vehicles and cartridges to the accused i.e., Manu Sharma, as well as his conduct after the incident prove his guilt beyond reasonable doubt.[17]

Senior advocate Ram Jethmalani, who represented Sharma in the Supreme Court, assailed the High Court verdict, alleging that the media had prejudged the issue and conducted a campaign to vilify his client. The Supreme Court accepted that there had been an element of "trial by media" but believed that it had not affected the decision of the High Court.

Media Coverage

Media attention grew as malpractices employed by Manu Sharma came to light. On 9 September 2006, a sting operation by the news magazine Tehelka was shown on the TV channel STAR News. This appeared to show that witnesses had been bribed and coerced into retracting their initial testimony. Venod Sharma was named in the exposé as one who had paid money to some of the witnesses. Facing pressure from the central Congress leaders, Venod Sharma resigned from the Haryana cabinet.[18]

"Bina Ramani had asked me to forget what happened since powerful people were involved" said the Jessica Lal's sister, for the first time, lashes out against the dubious role played by Bina Ramani and some senior police officials, including Amod Kanth, then joint commissioner. She also said that Bina Ramani did ask her and her family to forget about what had happened since powerful people were involved. She also told them that it may be dangerous for them since we did not know who they were dealing with, and they would not achieve anything by pursuing the case.[19]

The protest about the case also took place as the country's urban middle class rose in protest, angry at the inadequate law enforcement and the ease with which the rich and famous manipulated the courts.

University students sent SMS messages around New Delhi, urging citizens to rise up and protest against the faulty law system. The protestors wanted to get justice for Lal's death. They called the acquittal the "miscarriage of justice." A 24-hour news channel, NDTV, also started a campaign urging viewers to petition for a new trial. A few days after this campaign began, the station had received more than 200,000 cell phone text messages urging retrial. The Citizens went to the streets for marches and rallies. On 4 March 2006, students held a candlelight vigil at the capital's monument, India Gate. This action was inspired by a movie, "Rang de Basanti."[20]

On 7 March 2006, a pack of 150 college students poured onto Parliament Street in New Delhi to protest. They chanted "Jessica, Jessica" and pumped their fists. They also held up signs that read "Wake up from Ur Insane Slumber" and "We are in a country where you can get away if your dad is a politician." Surya, a Brazilian cosmetics company, passed out "Justice for Jessica" temporary tattoos. The company also ran a website, "Justice for Jessica" that produced names and e-mail addresses of thousands of Indians who registered their support for the protests[21].

Newspapers and televisions ran headlines that read "No one killed Jessica." In addition to the candlelight vigils that models, fashion designers, friends, and relatives held at India Gate, citizens held a week-long t-shirt campaign in which they wore t-shirts that read "we support re-investigation of Jessica Lal's murder, let the truth come out." In response to this media pressure and protests, the police, headed by Police Commissioner KK Paul, petitioned the High Court for a review of the case. On 22 March 2006, the court issued warrants against the nine defendants that had stood trial. On 9 September 2006, Tehelka, a news magazine, aired a show on the television that showed that witnesses had accepted bribes to retract their initial testimonies. Venod Sharma was a part of these bribes.

Parole

Manu Sharma was granted his first parole on 24 September 2009, for a *period of 30 days as he contended that he had to look after his family business, care for his ailing mother and attend the last rites* of his grandmother. His parole was extended for another 30 days during which he was seen attending parties in Delhi. His argument that he needed to attend to his ailing mother also fell apart after he was seen at a promotional event of a ladies cricket tournament in Chandigarh. Following an outcry, he returned to Tihar jail two weeks before his parole was to expire.

His second parole came in November 2011 when he said he wanted to attend the marriage of his younger brother. The 5-day parole was granted with strict restrictions on his movement. The parole also prevented him from visiting any nightclub.

In December 2013, Sharma was granted nine days parole to appear in examinations for a post-graduate degree in human rights. 30-day parole was also granted to him in December 2014 for his master's degree exams. He also was on 'furlough' in April 2015 when he married a Mumbai woman at his residence on April 22 with only close relatives from both sides invited to attend. Sharma was out on furlough and not parole which requires legal sanction. The official added that furlough is of usually up to two weeks and can be granted to a convict for "good conduct". While in jail, Sharma has also been involved with his NGO, Siddharth Vashisht Charitable Trust, which works for the welfare of jail inmates.

CONCLUSION

The Indian Judiciary suffers from chronic favouritism. So much so that the law is seen by many of the country's poor as a tool merely to be exercised by the rich and powerful. There have been numerous instances of high-profile law-breakers getting away with their mischief because of social influence. Even recently Salman Khan got bail in his case hours after being convicted in Mumbai even though thousands of ordinary jail inmates wait for years to get bail. The judiciary's willingness to bow to power and influence causes poor people to shun the legal process as much as possible.

In this light, the cases of Priyadarshani Mattoo and Jessica Lal show that when the call of justice is proactively raised by the public, the judiciary has the wherewithal to take prompt action.

The role of the media in bringing to fore the opinions of the public is crucial. The media as a conveyor of the public's mood is able to sway the decisions of people in power by making the public's voice heard. Without the role of media groups like NDTV and Tehelka, neither Santosh Singh nor Manu Sharma would have been brought to justice as promptly as they were. In both the cases, the High Court took serious note of the case only after intense media speculation. In the absence of the same, the reader may well imagine how long the trials might have stretched for.

Another regretful aspect of India's justice system is the woeful incompetence of most police personnel. In both Priyadarshani Matto's case and Jessica Lal's case, key police officials blundered at crucial stages of the investigation. Whether it was with regard to the recording of witness statements or collection of evidence, policemen in both the cases failed to do their duty. This was amply demonstrated in Priyadarshani Mattoo's case when the police called but refused to search for the servant who had seen Priyadarshani's killer near the site of the murder on the day of her death. Why is the police failing to do its job? The fault might lie with the training agencies rather than with the officers themselves. Police personnel are under-trained and therefore unable to accomplish basic tasks like recording witness statements. On top of that police officials are notoriously prone to be influenced by bribes and social clout. Such a lax attitude can only be changed if thorough changes are made in the police training process. If police personnel is trained well they would be more likely to be helpful in the investigation rather than become a hindrance as happened in these two cases.

END NOTES

1. Pinky Anand and Gauri Goburdhun, Trials of Truth: India's Landmark Criminal Cases (2018)
2. Albeena Shakil, The Priyadarsini Mattoo Case: Some lesions for the future, Contemporary Perspectives Jamia, 150, 150-154 (2007)
3. Ibid 2
4. State (through CBI) v Santosh Kumar Singh (2007), CriLJ, 964, 133(2006)DLT 393
5. Richa Srivastav, Case comment on Priya Darshini Matoo case, Legal Service India, http://www.legalservicesindia.com/article/644/case-comment-on-Priyadarshini-Matoo-case.html
6. Ibid 5
7. Outlook web Bureau, 11 Long years, Outlook India, Oct.17, 2006, https://www.outlookindia.com/website/story/11-long-years/232861
8. Supra note 4
9. Santosh Kumar Singh v State (2010) 9 SCC 747
10. Reporter, Priyadarsini Mattoo Case: HC gives 3-week Parole to Convict, The Hindu, May 15, 2019, https://www.thehindu.com/news/cities/Delhi/priyadarshini-mattoo-case-hc-gives-3-week-parole-to-convict/article 27131693.ece
11. Supra note 1
12. Lisette Alvarez, Justice for Jessica: A human rights case study on media influence, Rule of Law and Civic action in India, Florida State University Libraries (2011)
13. Michalis Kontopodis, Christos Varvantakis, Christoh Wulf, Global Youth in Digital Trajectories, 119-121 (2017)
14. Sidharth Vashisht @Manu Sharma v State (NCT Delhi), (2010), CRLA 179 (2007)
15. Rafiq Dossani, India Arring: How this economic power house is redefining global business, 78-79 (2007)
16. State (NCT Delhi) v Sidhartha Vashisht @Manu Sharma and Others, (2013), CRLA 193 (2006)
17. Samanta, Navajyoti, Trial by Media: Jessica Lal Case, SSRN (2008), https://ssrn.com/abstract=1003644 or http://dx.doi.org/10.2139/ssrn.1003644
18. Express Web Desk, What is Jessica Lal Murder Case?, The Indian Express, April 24, 2018, https://indianexpress.com/article/what-is/what-is-the-jessica-lal-murder-case/

19. Bhavna Vij-Aurora Interviews Sabrina Lall, The Outlook Magazine, April 10, 2006, https://www.outlookindia.com/magazine/story/bina-ramani-had-asked-me-to-forget-what-happened-since-powerful-people-were-inv/230864
20. AsmitaNandy, Jessica Lall Case: Murder, a Media Campaign, Justice & Forgiveness, The Quint, April 28, 2018, https://www.thequint.com/explainers/jessica-lall-case-sabrina-lall-on-manu-sharma-explainer
21. T.O. Aswathi, Media, *The Backbone Of Democracy: A Case Study Of Jessica Lal Murder Case*, 4 IJIRAS 398, 398-400 (2017)

SELECTED REFERENCES

Books

Pinky Anand and Gauri Goburdhun, *Trails of truth: India's Landmark criminal Cases* (2018)

Michalis Kontopodis, Christos Varvantakis, Christoph Wulf, *Global Youth in Digital Trajectories*, (2017)

Rafiq Dossani, *India Arriving: How this economic Power-House is Redefining Global Business*, (2007)

Journals/Articles

Albeena Shakil, *The Priyadarshini Mattoo Case: Some Lessons for the Future*, 1 Contemporary Perspectives Jamia 150, (2007)

Lisette Alvarez, *Justice for Jessica: A Human Rights Case Study on Media Influence*, Rule of Law, and Civic Action in India, Florida State University Libraries (2011)

Samanta, Navajyoti, *Trial by Media: Jessica Lal Case*, SSRN (2008)

Richa Srivastav, *Case Comment on Priyadarshini Matoo Case, Legal Service India*

T.O. Aswathi, Media, The Backbone Of Democracy: A Case Study Of Jessica Lal Murder Case, 4 IJIRAS 398, (2017)

Newspaper/Magazine

Reporter, Priyadarshini Mattoo Case: HC gives 3-week Parole to Convict, The Hindu, May 15, 2019, https://www.thehindu.com/news/cities/Delhi/priyadarshini-mattoo-case-hc-gives-3-week-parole-to-convict/article27131693.ece

Express Web Desk, What is Jessica Lal Murder Case?, The Indian Express, April 24, 2018, https://indianexpress.com/article/what-is/what-is-the-jessica-lal-murder-case/

Outlook Web Bureau, 11 Long Years, Outlook India, Oct. 17, 2006, https://www.outlookindia.com/website/story/11-long-years/232861

Bhavna Vij-Aurora Interviews Sabrina Lall, The Outlook Magazine, April 10, 2006, https://www.outlookindia.com/magazine/story/bina-ramani-had-asked-me-to-forget-what-happened-since-powerful-people-were-inv/230864

AsmitaNandy, Jessica Lall Case: Murder, a Media Campaign, Justice & Forgiveness, The Quint, April 28, 2018, https://www.thequint.com/explainers/jessica-lall-case-sabrina-lall-on-manu-sharma-explainer

Index

□□□